KINGFISHER POCKET GUIDES
ASTRONOMY

Written by
JAMES MUIRDEN

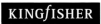

KINGFISHER
Kingfisher Publications Plc
New Penderel House
283–288 High Holborn
London WC1V 7HZ
www.kingfisherpub.com

This edition first published by
Kingfisher Publications Plc 2002

10 9 8 7 6 5 4 3 2 1
1TR/1201/WKT/-(MAR)/128KMALG

A CIP catalogue record for this book is available from the
British Library

ISBN 0 7534 0743 4

Senior Editor : Michèle Byam
Assistant Editor : Mandy Cleeve
Design : Smiljka Surla
Cover design : Mike Davis

Colour separations : P+W Graphics, Singapore
Printed in Hong Kong

Contents

Introduction

A stronomy is a science, but it is also an exciting voyage of discovery. The sky is free for all to see, town-dwellers and country-dwellers alike. Everything, from the blinding Sun to the dimmest star, waits to be discovered.

Just as there are different kinds of object in the sky, so there are different types of astronomer. Some are referred to rather contemptuously by their more active cousins as 'armchair' astronomers

▶ **Some of the stars** in this photograph are more luminous than the Sun, and others are dimmer. They all belong to the Milky Way galaxy, a vast collection of about 400 billion stars. The filmy clouds of gas and dust, or nebulae, will one day form clusters of new stars.

▼ **The 3.9-metre** Anglo-Australian reflecting telescope, New South Wales: one of the modern 'giants'.

as they get most of their enjoyment from reading and looking at pictures. But true amateur astronomy involves looking at the sky.

Amateurs and Professionals
Contrary to popular belief, the great majority of amateur astronomers do not possess a large telescope. Binoculars are the commonest astronomical instrument. Some enthusiasts do indeed

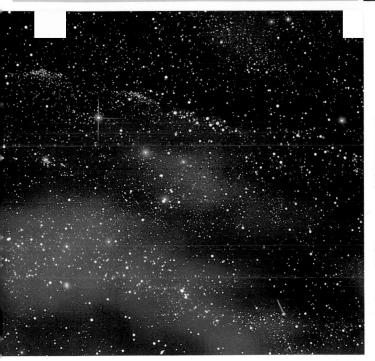

have an observatory in their gardens; but it is worth remembering that important discoveries have been made with the naked eye alone. After all, the ancient astronomers – in Greece, China and Egypt – gathered information with the simplest sighting instruments. Their method was to observe the sky and keep detailed records of everything they saw.

Professional astronomers today, of course, have the use of massive telescopes and other sophisticated equipment. For them the sky is literally the limit. Some amateurs go on to become professionals, but then a curious thing happens: they stop gazing upwards and spend their time looking at dots on photographs or in the company of unromantic computers. So this book is for true amateurs, who want to go out beneath the sky and begin their voyage of astronomical discovery.

The Amateur Astronomer

Many amateur astronomers start out as star-gazers who regularly scan the night sky, making themselves familiar with the stars and their patterns. Some amateurs become particularly interested in the bodies that make up our solar system: the Sun, Moon, planets, comets and other smaller objects. Other prefer to look much further into space, examining the stars, star clusters and gaseous nebulae belonging to the Milky Way or Galaxy. They even search out other galaxies, so distant that light takes millions of years on its journey.

◀ **The constellations of Gemini**, the Twins (top) and Orion (right) are familiar winter constellations to amateur astronomers. They are shown here over the city of Vancouver, Canada.

▶ **Comet West**, seen here in 1976, was one of the brightest comets of the century, and some observers saw the brilliant nucleus in daylight. It was one of the many comets discovered by a small band of amateurs who continuously search the night sky for these fleeting visitors.

▼ **The Moon's surface** has been thoroughly surveyed by spacecraft, but amateurs never tire of gazing at its mountains and craters.

Amateur Discoveries

Important discoveries are sometimes made by amateurs, even in these days of giant telescopes. Some are made relatively near at hand; others out in remote regions of space. On Christmas evening 1980, for example, an English enthusiast, Roy Panther, discovered a new comet using a home-made telescope. More recently, on February 19, 1992, an American amateur, Peter Collins, was surveying the Milky Way when he noticed a nova – an exploding star – among the thousands of other faint points of light. In Australia, the Reverend Robert Evans has discovered more than 25 exploding stars in galaxies far away from our own Milky Way.

The Amateur Astronomer

Equipment – Binoculars

You can enjoy many hours of observation and see thousands of stars with no equipment at all, and this is how most amateurs start out. But binoculars and telescopes are useful. They allow you to see more objects in the sky and to examine them in more detail.

Binoculars

Binoculars consist of a pair of identical small telescopes with their light paths 'folded' to make them more compact. Although they are not as powerful as a true astronomical telescope, they have the great advantage of portability and comfortable viewing with both eyes.

An ordinary pair of binoculars will reveal about 30 stars for every single star seen with the naked eye. But they must be held steadily, which means resting them – or your elbows – on a solid support. Otherwise the stars will jump about, due to your heartbeat and muscular tension.

Binoculars do not provide very high magnification, so they will not reveal planetary details, although good ones will show three or four satellites of Jupiter and the crescent phase of Venus. They will also show the larger craters on the Moon, and through them sunspots can be projected on to a sheet of paper.

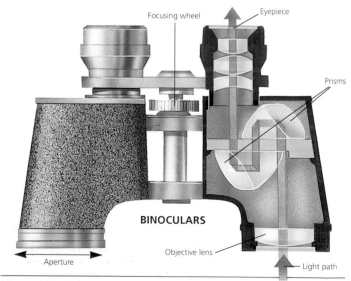

Focusing wheel

Eyepiece

Prisms

BINOCULARS

Aperture

Objective lens

Light path

The Amateur Astronomer

Aperture and Magnification

Binoculars and small hand telescopes belong to the same family of low-power instruments. The most important features are the *aperture* and the *magnification*. The aperture is the diameter of the objective lens at the front of the instrument – which is usually between 30 and 50 millimetres. The larger this lens is, the brighter is the image of a star, since more light is being collected.

The magnification indicates how much larger an object looks. The Moon is half a degree across in the sky; through a x 10 telescope it will look five degrees across. The higher the magnification, the smaller is the amount of sky that can be seen at any one time.

Binoculars carry labels such as 8 x 30 and 10 x 50. In the first case, the magnification is x 8 and the objective is 30 millimetres across; the second has a magnification of x 10 and an aperture of 50 millimetres. For general astronomical work a 10 x 50 instrument is ideal. Higher magnifications are difficult to hold steady.

Refracting Telescopes

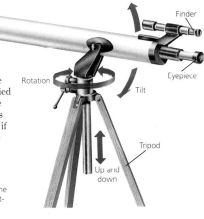

Most telescopes are refractors: that is to say, they have an objective lens to collect and focus the light and form an image of the object near the other end of the tube (see the diagram below). This image is magnified by a small lens called the *eyepiece*. The objective lens should contain two glass components, one in front of the other; if a single lens is used, the image will be coloured and blurred. A two-lens objective is said to be *achromatic*, or colour-free.

▼ **A typical modern** refracting telescope. The small finder helps to locate objects. The light-path through the telescope is shown below.

13

The Amateur Astronomer

The smallest useful refractor for astronomical purposes has an aperture of 60 millimetres, but 75 millimetres is much better, and anything larger is really powerful. A refractor's tube is usually about fifteen times as long as the aperture, and this is one disadvantage: refractors are not easy to mount rigidly. Many cheap refractors not only give poor definition, but are mounted on wobbly stands. A poorly-mounted telescope is useless, since no detail can be seen if the image vibrates. Nights when the air is damp and still often give fine views. However, dew on optical surfaces can be a problem, and refractors are more affected than reflectors, because the objective lens is so exposed. A cylindrical 'dew cap' made of black card, extending for about three times the aperture in front of the lens, will help to keep the glass bright.

BUYING A TELESCOPE

When buying any telescope, try to get an experienced observer to have a look through it before you finally decide. Get in touch with your local astronomical society about this (see page 172); they will be delighted to help. A poor telescope could turn you off astronomy before you have even begun!

Most telescopes are supplied with several eyepieces. To find the magnification, divide the focal length of the eyepiece (which should be marked) into the focal length of the objective (the distance from the lens to the image it forms of a distant object). Three magnifications are best, for example:

Aperture	Magnifications		
60 mm	x 30	x 90	x 150
80 mm	x 40	x 120	x 200
100 mm	x 50	x 150	x 250

Low powers show more of the sky at one time. High powers are needed for fine details.

▼ **Two early telescopes.** In front, the long tube of one of Galileo's refractors, made in 1610. It was with this or a similar instrument that he discovered four of Jupiter's moons, Saturn's rings and the Moon's craters. Behind it is an 18th-century reflecting telescope, with its mirrors arranged so that the observer looked 'up' the tube as with a refractor.

◄ **The 1-metre refractor** of Yerkes Observatory, Wisconsin, USA, is the world's largest. The glass for the huge lens was cast for another projected instrument, which had to be abandoned.

The Amateur Astronomer

Reflecting Telescopes

Reflecting telescopes are used only by astronomers. Their attraction over refractors is that large mirrors are cheaper to produce than lenses of the same size. They are also more compact than refractors and can therefore be mounted more easily. The smallest commercially-available reflectors have a concave mirror about 100 millimetres across. But the best size for an amateur is 150 millimetres. A good telescope of this size can give a lifetime of enjoyment.

To give good definition, the mirrors in a reflecting telescope need to be polished accurately within about one tenth of the wavelength of visible light, or about 0.00005 millimetre of perfection. A Newtonian (see below) consists of a concave mirror of parabolic cross-section, and a small flat mirror to reflect the focused light through a hole in the side of the tube. A Cassegrain (also below) has a small convex mirror

which sends the light back through the small hole cut in the main mirror.

Other more complicated reflectors have been developed but the Newtonian is the one most amateurs use. The Cassegrain type is much more expensive. Astronomical mirrors are usually coated with aluminium on the front surface. These coatings must be replaced occasionally and this is the main drawback of reflectors.

Some amateurs have made reflecting telescopes with apertures of 500 mm or more. Because they are so compact, it is possible to mount even very large instruments on simple plywood stands that can be easily transported.

Another popular type of telescope is basically a Cassegrain, but uses a large lens at the front of the tube as well as a pair of mirrors. Known as a 'catadioptric' telescope, it has an extremely short tube and is therefore very portable.

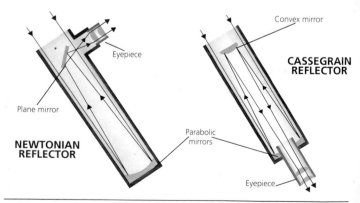

Eyepiece

Plane mirror

NEWTONIAN REFLECTOR

Convex mirror

CASSEGRAIN REFLECTOR

Parabolic mirrors

Eyepiece

TELESCOPE MOUNTINGS

Telescopes are generally mounted in one of two ways. The simplest is the *altazimuth* mounting. This allows the tube to move vertically and horizontally. To follow a star you have to swivel the telescope up and around little by little and this can be awkward.

An *equatorial* mounting avoids this problem, allowing you to follow the path of a star with just one movement. It has two axes at right angles to each other like the altazimuth but one is parallel to the Earth's axis. If this (the polar axis) is turned once a day opposite to the direction in which the Earth spins, the telescope keeps pointing in the same direction (see the diagram on the right). The other axis – the declination axis – is used only when locating an object to begin with.

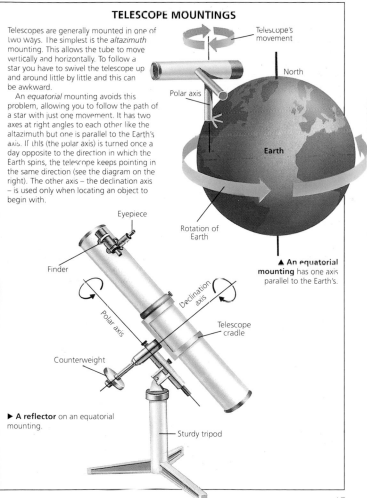

Telescope's movement

North

Polar axis

Earth

Rotation of Earth

▲ **An equatorial mounting** has one axis parallel to the Earth's.

Eyepiece

Finder

Declination axis

Polar axis

Telescope cradle

Counterweight

▶ **A reflector** on an equatorial mounting.

Sturdy tripod

The Amateur Astronomer

Almost all professional instruments are reflectors; the last big refractor, the one-metre telescope at Yerkes, USA, was built in 1897.

Many amateurs have built their own reflectors, using purchased optics and making the tube and mounting. This is certainly the cheapest way of obtaining a powerful telescope, for anyone with a workshop and some skill in using tools.

Magnification

The illustration on the right gives you an idea of what an amateur can expect to see. If you hold the book about 25 centimetres away, it shows the planets as seen through a telescope magnifying 200 times. Each planet is shown near its maximum and minimum possible distance from the Earth (Uranus, Neptune and Pluto are omitted).

But the telescopic view is never as steady as this; currents in the atmosphere make the image flicker and blur. And a small telescope will reveal less detail than a large one.

A Telescope's View

Most astronomical telescopes give an upside-down view. Terrestrial telescopes use extra lenses to give an upright image. Astronomers do without these because any piece of glass in the light beam makes the image fainter.

◀ **The large dome here** houses one of the world's largest telescopes: the 4-metre Mayall reflector on Kitt Peak, Arizona. Although telescopes in airless space can obtain much sharper images than those on the Earth, there are still many important observing programmes that can be carried out at ground level, and very large telescopes are still being planned.

Minimum   Maximum

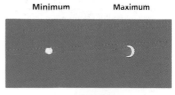

MERCURY

VENUS

MARS

JUPITER

SATURN

The base from which we observe the sky is moving all the time – but we are so used to living on the spinning Earth that we assume it is stationary, and that everything in the universe moves around it. We seem, like the observer in the diagram below, to be at the centre of a huge rotating invisible sphere – the celestial sphere. The heavenly bodies seem to be attached to the inside of this sphere and carried around it in an east to west direction.

Since the Earth revolves on its north-south axis, the celestial sphere appears to rotate around the same axis. If a camera is directed towards one of the celestial poles, and the shutter is left open for a few minutes while the Earth spins, the stars form trails centred on the pole.

Ptolemy's Universe

The illusion that the stars, planets and Sun revolve around the Earth is so convincing that people believed in it for thousands of years. The Greek astronomer Ptolemy (about AD 140) worked out a complicated system in which the different planets, the Sun, Moon and stars, all had their own invisible shells or spheres rotating around the Earth. These separate spheres were necessary because only the stars keep the same relative positions from night to night. The planets and the Moon wander across the sky.

◀ **This 40-minute exposure** shows the sky turning about the north celestial pole.

▼ **The celestial sphere**. A celestial object is highest when it crosses the meridian.

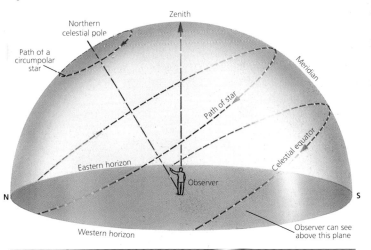

Zenith

Northern celestial pole

Path of a circumpolar star

Meridian

Path of star

Celestial equator

Eastern horizon

Observer

N

S

Western horizon

Observer can see above this plane

The Moving Sky

The Spinning Earth

Today we know that the Earth and everything we see is moving. The stars appear in the same place but they are not stationary. Some are moving very fast, but they are so far away that their position in relation to each other does not seem to change. The planets are nearer and their movement more noticeable. They revolve around the Sun and so their positions on the celestial

sphere slowly change. The Moon takes only a month to go round the celestial sphere once. The Sun takes a year – the length of time taken by the Earth to complete one orbit.

▼ **The planets** appear to move around the celestial sphere in an irregular manner, simply because the Earth also moves. In Ptolemy's Earth-centred universe, these irregularities had to be explained by supposing each planet to move in a small epicycle, as shown here.

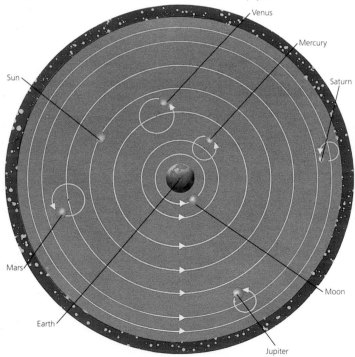

PROVING THE EARTH'S ROTATION

Jean Foucault's famous experiment to prove that the Earth rotates was carried out in Paris in 1851. He hung a iron ball on a wire about 61 metres long (see above). A heavy weight tends to keep swinging in the same direction while the Earth turns underneath it, making the pendulum's direction appear to change.

It is possible to carry out this experiment with a long thread and a weight. The longer the thread, the better, and the weight should be a heavy as possible. A good place to hang the thread is at the top of a staircase but draughts, vibrations and twists in the thread must be avoided if the pendulum is to keep swinging in the same plane. Mark the path of the pendulum at the start on a simple grid and return later to observe the apparent change of direction.

Thread (at least 6 metres long)

◄ **A pendulum** needs to keep swinging on its own, protected from draughts, for about half an hour before the Earth's rotation is noticeable. The thread (nylon fishing line is suitable) should be at least 6 metres long and be capable of supporting a weight of at least 5 kilograms. At intervals draw lines AB on a sheet of paper to show its changed direction.

Weight (at least 5 kilogrammes)

A

B

23

The Moving Sky

THE APPARENT PATH OF ORION

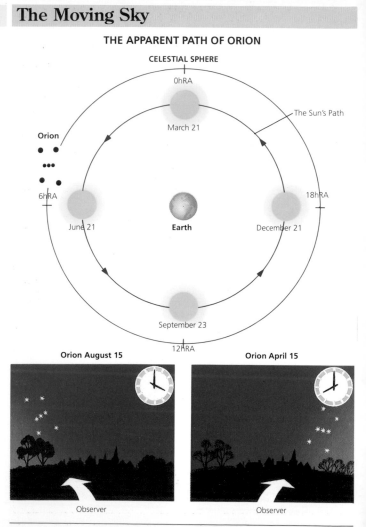

CELESTIAL SPHERE

0hRA

March 21

The Sun's Path

Orion

6hRA

June 21

Earth

18hRA

December 21

September 23

12hRA

Orion August 15

Observer

Orion April 15

Observer

24

Constellations and the Seasons

The Earth's annual journey around the Sun makes our star appear to travel round the celestial sphere once in a year. This affects the visibility of the constellations, since stars cannot be seen in the daytime.

Look, for example, at the diagram on the left. It shows the apparent movement of the Sun as the Earth orbits, and the famous constellation of Orion. In June the Sun lies in the direction of Orion, which is therefore in the daytime sky and invisible. By August, however, the Earth's oribital motion has carried the

Sun some way east of Orion and it now rises in the morning sky before dawn. By midwinter, the Sun appears opposite Orion in the sky, and the constellation is well placed for midnight viewing. By April, the Sun has moved in close on its western side, and Orion disappears into the evening twilight once more.

This is the same for almost all the constellations. Because of the Earth's movement around the Sun, each is visible at different times of the year – some only in winter, others only in summer.

THE SEASONS

If the Earth's axis were upright the Sun would pass directly over the equator every day. But the axis is tilted in a fixed direction, 23½° from the vertical.

On June 21, the north pole is inclined towards the Sun, bringing midsummer to the northern hemisphere, while the south

experiences midwinter. On December 21 the situation is reversed, while spring and autumn occur between these times.

With a clear view of the horizon, record the changing sunrise or sunset point during the year. At the equinoxes, the Sun rises exactly in the east and sets exactly in the west.

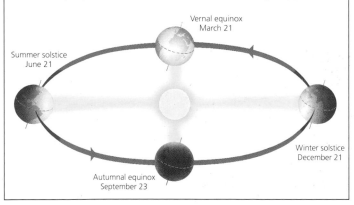

Summer solstice
June 21

Vernal equinox
March 21

Winter solstice
December 21

Autumnal equinox
September 23

The Moving Sky

Solar Days and Sidereal Days

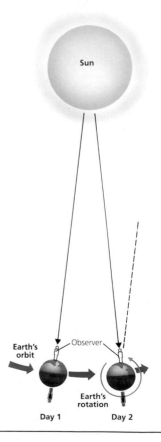

Light from Stars

Sun

Earth's orbit

Observer

Earth's rotation

Day 1   Day 2

Since life on Earth is regulated by day and night, the Sun is used as the basic timekeeper. The normal Sun or *solar* day corresponds to the interval between successive noons or midnights – that is the 24 hours in which the Earth spins once on it axis.

But as the Earth orbits the Sun at the same time as it spins, the solar day does not indicate the true rotation of the Earth in space with respect to the stars.

Look at the diagram on the right. On Day 1 it is noon to one observer and midnight to the other. One *sidereal* day later (Day 2), it is not quite noon and midnight again, since the Earth has moved a little way along its orbit, and must spin slightly more to bring the Sun back to where it was.

Since most astronomers observe the Moon, planets and stars, their telescopes are adjusted to turn on their polar axis in one sidereal day (23h 56m), the time the celestial sphere takes to rotate once. The amateur must remember that each month the constellations will be in the same positions two hours earlier and that every night the stars appear to rise four minutes earlier. On page 65, you will find how Sidereal Time indicates which constellations are well placed for observation.

The position of a city or river on Earth can be found on a map using latitude and longitude. The position of an object on the celestial sphere is also described in these terms but latitude is called *Declination* or *Dec* and longitude *Right Ascension* or *RA*. These are the celestial or astronomical co-ordinates.

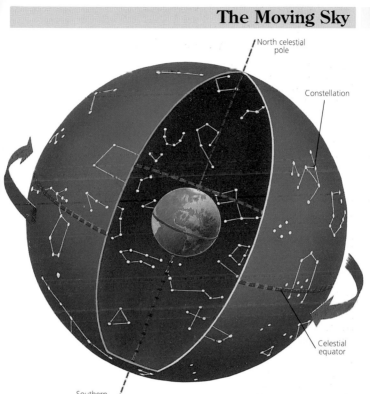

North celestial
pole

Constellation

Celestial
equator

Southern
celestial pole

CELESTIAL CO-ORDINATES

Declination is reckoned in degrees north (positive) or south (negative) of the celestial equator – the line dividing the celestial sphere into two halves, in the plane of the Earth's equator.

Right Ascension is divided into 24 sidereal hours, measured eastwards from 0h, which is the RA of the Sun on the first day of northern spring (March 21).

The Sidereal Time is equal to the RA that is due south (or due north to a southern observer) at any instant, and is shown by special astronomical clocks.

The Moving Sky

Constellations and the Sun

The celestial equator and poles are useful for defining the grid of celestial latitude and longitude, but they are not of any 'astronomical' importance. They simply corespond to the way our insignificant Earth spins. The significant plane is the *ecliptic*.

The ecliptic is the plane of the Earth's orbit. If the Sun was dimmer than the Full Moon, so that the stars could be seen during the day, the ecliptic could be plotted on the celestial sphere by noting the Sun's position in front of the stars during the course of a whole year. (An equally good method, if it were possible, would be to stand on the Sun and observe the annual course of the Earth in front of the stars.) Once plotted in this way, it is found that the plane of

the ecliptic crosses the plane of the equator at an angle of 23½ degrees.

The orbital planes of the Moon and planets coincide fairly closely with that of the Earth. They are always to be found within a few degrees of the ecliptic, in a band known as the *Zodiac*. The word means 'circle of animals' and refers to the constellations: Aries, Taurus, Gemini, Cancer, Leo, Virgo, Libra, Scorpius, Sagittarius, Capricornus, Aquarius and Pisces. These star groups make up the

▼ **This map shows** the Sun's path or ecliptic around the celestial sphere. Its position on the first day of each month is indicated by a yellow circle. The planets are always to be found within the 18° band, the Zodiac, centred on the ecliptic.

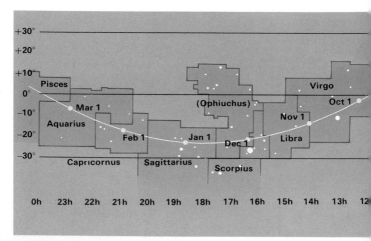

The Moving Sky

sequence of constellations through
which the Sun, Moon and planets
all pass.

At the beginning of summer in the
northern hemisphere, the Sun lies on
the borders of Taurus and Gemini.
At the beginning of winter it lies
in the constellation Sagittarius.
It crosses the celestial equator
in the constellations of Pisces
(at the beginning of spring) and
in Virgo (at the beginning of
autumn). In the southern
hemisphere, these positions
represent the opposite seasons.

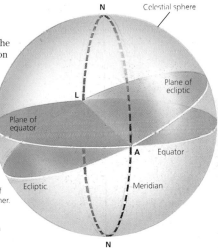

▶ **This diagram** shows how the planes of
the equator and the ecliptic cross each other.
The points marked L and A are called the
equinoxes, and the Sun occupies these
positions at the beginning of the northern
autumn and spring respectively.

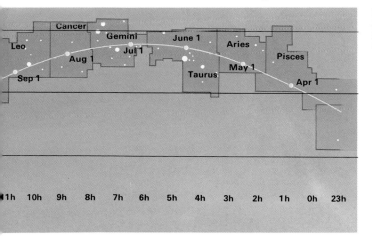

The Sun – Our Star

There is nothing strange about the Sun, apart from its closeness. It is about a quarter of a million times nearer to us than the next known star, which means that we can examine it in far more detail than any of its neighbours. Solar astronomy is a particularly important subject, and amateur observers can enjoy studying the Sun's surface provided that they take proper precautions (see pages 36 and 37).

Remember that you must never look directly at the Sun.

Long before serious astronomy began, the Sun's daily motion across the sky and annual movement around the celestial sphere were studied. Farmers, for example, would use the Sun's position to tell them when they should plant crops. As has been shown on page 25, the seasons are caused by the Earth being tilted on its axis. This also affects

SUN FACTS

Diameter: 1,392,000 kilometres
(109 X Earth)
Mass: 328,000 X Earth
Volume: 1,300,000 X Earth
Surface temperature:
5500°C
Core temperature:
about 15,000,000°C
True equatorial rotation period:
25.38 days
Apparent equatorial rotation period:
27.28 days
Mean distance from Earth:
149,600,000 kilometres
Cosmic year (time to orbit Galaxy):
225 million years
Estimated age:
4600 million years

the position of the Sun around the year. In winter it never rises as high in the sky as it does in summer, and the points on the horizon at which it rises and sets shift with the seasons.

This changing position of sunrise and sunset throughout the year gave early civilizations the basis of a calendar. They must have realized that these positions repeated themselves, so that natural or artifical markers could be used to decide the time when different seasons began. Stonehenge, England, is the most famous structure to determine the moment of midsummer sunrise.

▼ **The Sun's daily path** across the sky changes with the seasons of the year.

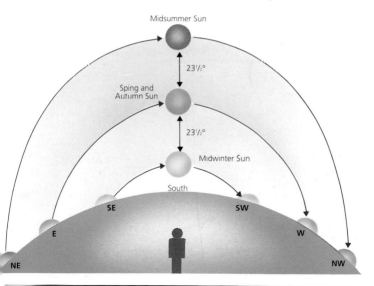

Midsummer Sun

Spring and
Autumn Sun

23½°

23½°

Midwinter Sun

South

SE

SW

E

W

NE

NW

The Sun – Our Star

Time and the Sun

The shadow cast by a sundial indicates the approximate time of day. It is rarely exactly right, because the Sun wanders several degrees east and west of its 'true' position.

This happens mainly because the Earth's orbit is slightly elliptical, and its orbital velocity varies, making the Sun appear to move fast or slow. Clocks are therefore regulated to Mean Solar Time, known as Greenwich Mean Time (GMT) or Universal Time (UT). The difference between this and sundial time (or Apparent Solar time) is known as the *equation of time* (see right).

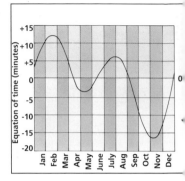

Simple Sundials

The simplest sundials consists of an upright stick in the ground. When the shadow points exactly north (or south, in the southern hemisphere), it is Apparent Noon. The equation of time correction will give True Noon, but this will only agree with Mean Solar Time if the sundial is exactly on one of the world's standard meridians.

In summer, the shadow cast by the stick is shorter than it is in winter. If the position of the shadow's tip is marked at True Noon every few days throughout the year, a shape like that shown below, the *analemma*, will be produced. Use this graph to determine true local time from a sundial. In the green area, add the equation of time to the dial's shadow reading; in the brown area, subtract it.

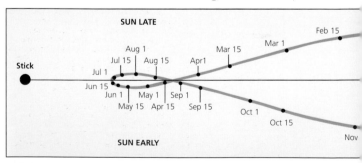

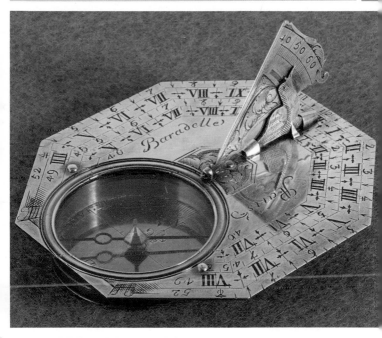

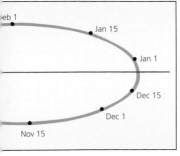

Feb 1
Jan 15
Jan 1
Dec 15
Dec 1
Nov 15

▲ **A sundial's gnomon**, which casts the shadow, has to be parallel with the Earth's axis. This means that its altitude is equal to the latitude, and it is aligned north-south. In the portable sundial seen here, a magnetic compass and level are used to adjust it before a reading is taken. The altitude of the gnomon is adjustable for use in different latitudes, and the time is read off the horizontal plate.

◀ **A shape like that on the left** is known as the analemma. This is the locus of the tip of the noonday shadow cast by a stick throughout the year. The higher the latitude on the Earth's surface, the more elongated the analemma becomes.

The Sun – Our Star

Sunspots and the Solar Cycle

The Sun has shone steadily for thousands of millions of years, but its surface, the *photosphere*, does not always look the same. Dark spots come and go and the number visible follows a cycle of about 11 years. This cycle also affects the shape of the Sun's faint atmosphere, or *corona*, which can be seen only during a total eclipse.

A sunspot is caused by a very strong magnetic field generated from the swirling material beneath the photosphere. Radiation from the interior is sucked away, leaving a cooler, darker area above. Sunspot interiors are about a thousand degrees cooler than the photosphere, but they are still hotter than the surfaces of many stars, and appear dark only by contrast.

If the image of a dark sunspot is projected on to a screen, it is seen to consist of a dark centre (the *umbra*) and a lighter surrounding area (the *penumbra*). Many spots occur in pairs, and a large group lasts for several weeks or even months, and may be ten times the Earth's diameter in extent. At maximum activity, a dozen different groups may be visible at the same time and, as the Sun rotates, new sunspots come into view.

▼ **Sunspot groups** such as these are several times larger than the Earth. Their frequency rises and falls every 11 years, but even at `minimum' activity there are usually some small spots visible.

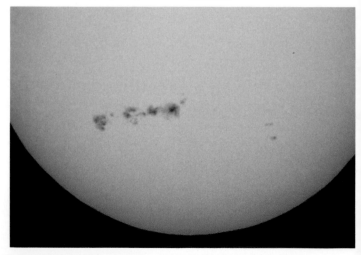

▼ **These drawings** of the Sun were made by projecting its image with binoculars at an interval of two days. The dotted line represents its equator.

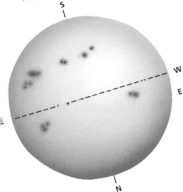

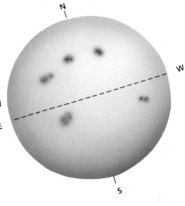

▼ **The Sun** being viewed by projection, using binoculars. A simple wooden stand helps to keep the image sharp and steady.

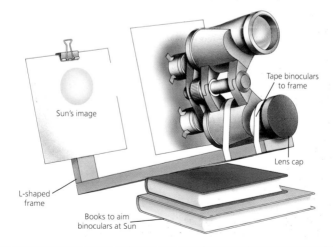

Sun's image

Tape binoculars to frame

Lens cap

L-shaped frame

Books to aim binoculars at Sun

The Sun – Our Star

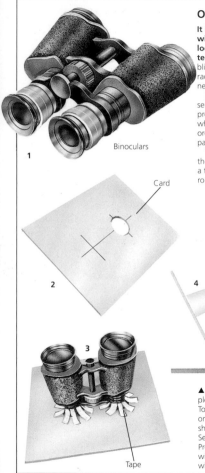

Binoculars

Card

2

OBSERVING THE SUN

It is highly dangerous to look at the Sun with the naked eye and you must never look at the Sun directly through telescopes or binoculars. People have been blinded in this way. The Sun's awesome radiation will destroy the eye's sensitive nerves in seconds.

Fortunately, there is a perfectly safe and sensible way of observing sunspots: by projecting the solar image on to a sheet of white paper. This can be done using an ordinary telescope (refractor of reflector), or a pair of binoculars.

The white paper is held some way behind the eyepiece (about 30 centimetres will do for a trial), and the eyepiece is adjusted until the round image of the Sun is sharp. The size of

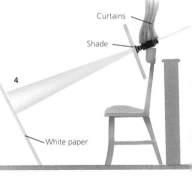

Curtains

Shade

4

White paper

3

Tape

▲ **A pair of binoculars** like these can reveal plenty of sunspots (1).
To make a shade, draw the outline of the lenses on a piece of card and cut out one of the shapes as shown (2).
Secure the card with tape (3).
Prop the binoculars on a chair by the window and focus the Sun's image on to a while screen (4).

the solar image can be increased by moving the screen further back from the eyepiece.

The image must be screened from direct light, or its details will be washed out. A projection box (right), with a hole cut in the side to reveal the image, gives a very bright view. But even a simple shade will be adequate. A viewing box is particularly useful if a highly-magnified image is being projected, because it improves the contrast of the much fainter image.

It is fascinating to watch a sunspot group develop from day to day: keep an eye on the Sun's eastern limb, because this is where its rotation carries new groups into view. You can keep a useful record of solar activity simply by counting the number of groups that are visible every day.

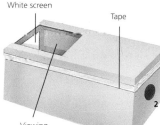

White screen

Tape

1

Viewing aperture

2

Sun's image

3

▲ **For solar projection** with a telescope a shoe box works well. Cut a hole in one end, to take the tube (1).
Stick a white screen at the other end, and cut out a viewing aperture (2).
Fit the box to the tube, and focus the image (3).

The Sun – Our Star

Observation Notes

Observing sunspots is, or should be, a daily business. The simplest method is to count the groups that are visible. After each month, add up the total number of groups observed and divide this by the number of days on which observations were made. The result is the Mean Daily Frequency (MDF) for the month.

Another interesting project is to draw the solar disc with its spots. The easiest way is to make a projection grid (below) and focus the Sun's image on to it. Note the positions of the spots on the grid. Then copy them on to a sheet of thin paper, bearing the Sun's circular outline, laid over an identical grid so that the lines show through.

Before starting, however, you must fix the cardinal points on the disc. Leave the telescope fixed, and let the Sun's image drift across the screen. Twist the grid so that the sunspot trails accurately along the east-west line, and you know that the image is orientated correctly. Most astronomical telescopes give an inverted view.

▼ **It is not always easy** to tell which is north, south, east or west on the Sun! These two pictures show the orientation of the projected image using binoculars (top) and an inverting astronomical telescope (below). Observers in the southern hemisphere should reverse these directions. It helps to remember that the Sun drifts towards the west.

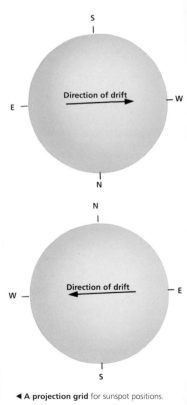

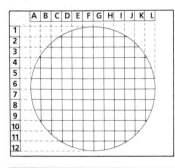

◀ **A projection grid** for sunspot positions.

Solar Eclipses

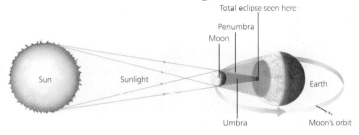

Total eclipse seen here

Penumbra

Moon

Sun

Sunlight

Earth

Umbra

Moon's orbit

B y a coincidence, the Sun and Moon appear about the same size in the sky. When the Moon passes in front of the Sun, it can block out the solar disc completely. Darkness falls, and the faint outer atmosphere or corona shines out around the black lunar outline during the seconds or minutes that the total eclipse lasts (see photograph on right).

To see a total eclipse, you must be within the Moon's shadow as it sweeps over the Earth's surface, and this shadow is rarely more than a few hundred kilometres wide. Outside the central shadow, or umbra, is the wide penumbra, in which only a partial eclipse is seen.

In addition to the pale corona, the

red prominences – colossal eruptions of hot gas, many times the size of the Earth – can often be seen shining around the edge of the Moon. Such a sight is well worth a long journey!

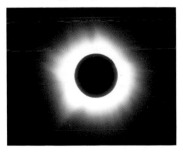

TOTAL SOLAR ECLIPSE TABLE		
Date	**Maximum duration**	**Area of Visibility**
1995 Oct 24	2m 5s	Iran, India, East Indies, Pacific Ocean
1997 Mar 8–9	2m 50s	East Asia, Japan, USA
1998 Feb 26	4m 9s	USA, Central and South America, Atlantic Ocean
1999 Aug 11	2m 23s	USA, W. Europe, Africa, Asia
2001 Jun 21	4m 57s	South America, Atlantic Ocean, Africa
2002 Dec 4	2m 4s	South Africa, Australia

The Stars

When the stars shine out on a clear night, the sight is both confusing and awe-inspiring. Any attempt to organize them into constellations appears hopeless. The only definite first impression you may have is that some stars are very bright, while others can only be glimpsed.

In fact, this simple observation raises an important issue. Suppose that the stars have the same true brightness or luminosity. Then the faint ones must be more remote than the bright ones, just as a nearby street-lamp outshines one further down the road. But if instead you suppose that the stars are equally distant, then the bright-looking ones must really be more luminous than the faint ones.

The early astronomers, who believed that the stars were attached to an invisible sphere, clearly held the second opinion. But one of the first men to study the stars seriously, William Herschel (who in 1781 discovered the planet Uranus), worked on the assumption that the stars are all equally luminous, and tried to gauge their relative distances by measuring their brightness in the sky.

Neither simple theory is correct. Some stars are over a million times more luminous than others, while the closest ones are thousands of times nearer than the most remote that have been detected in the Galaxy. But luminous stars are more conspicuous, simply because they can be seen at greater distances.

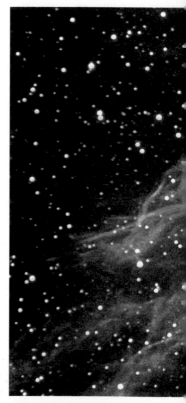

▶ **The Veil Nebula** in Cygnus, an enormous 'bubble' of material from an ancient star explosion. It now measures about five times the Moon's diameter in the sky.

Brightness and Magnitude

The brightness of a star is measured in *magnitudes*. One magnitude step means a brightness ratio of 2·512. This number is chosen so that a 5-magnitude difference corresponds to a brightness ratio of exactly 100. In other words a 6th magnitude star is exactly 100 times fainter than a 1st magnitude star. The larger the number, the fainter the star. Stars that are brighter than magnitude 0 stars are given a negative magnitude.

Apparent magnitude indicates a star's brightness in the sky. The original apparent magnitude scale was developed by the astronomer Hipparchos in 130 BC, who called the faintest naked-eye stars magnitude 6 (often written mag 6), and the brightest stars magnitude 1. His rough estimates were greatly refined when light-measuring methods were

The Stars

developed, and the scale was extended through 0 into negative numbers. The brightest star in the sky, Sirius, has an apparent magnitude of -1·47. The faintest stars detectable with a 150-millimetre telescope are about magnitude 13, or over 600,000 times fainter than Sirius.

Observing in Mediterranean skies, the 6th-magnitude stars of Hipparchos are much dimmer than the faintest visible to modern observers living in cities and urban areas, who may not be able to make out anything dimmer than

▼ **The patterns** that the stars make in the sky do not reveal their distribution in space. The stars forming the constellation of Orion appear to be projected on the celestial sphere in the pattern shown below left. In fact they are at very different distances from the Sun as shown in the illustration below right. (Imagine that the Sun is located below the illustration).

the 3rd magnitude. The principal cause is not dust and dirt, which is far less than in the coal-burning age, but 'light pollution' – artificial light directed up into the air. This brightens the night sky by illuminating hydrocarbons from vehicle exhausts and industrial waste.

Absolute magnitude indicates a star's luminosity; it is the apparent magnitude it would have if viewed from a distance of 32·6 light-years. (A light-year (l.y.) is the distance light travels in one year: about nine and a half million kilometres.) The most luminous known stars are about magnitude -7. The Sun's absolute magnitude is 4·8 – about 40,000 times fainter. However, some nearby stars of about a millionth of the Sun's luminosity have been detected, so that it does lie in the upper half of the brightness table.

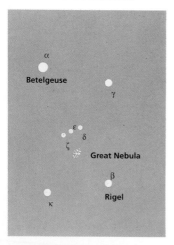

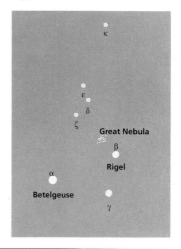

THE BRIGHTEST STARS IN THE SKY

| Star | Constellation | Magnitude | | Type | Distance |
		App.	Abs.		(l.y.)
Sirius (α)	Canis Major	-1.47	1.4	Dwarf	8.7
Canopus (α)	Carina	-0.7	-8.5	Supergiant	1200
Rigel Kent (α)	Centaurus	-0.3	4.4	Dwarf	910
Arcturus (α)	Boötes	-0.1	-0.3	Giant	36
Vega (α)	Lyra	0.0	0.6	Dwarf	26
Rigel (β)	Orion	0.1	-7.0	Supergiant	850
Capella (α)	Auriga	0.1	0.3	Giant	45
Procyon (α)	Canis Minor	0.3	2.6	Subgiant	11
Achernar (α)	Eridanus	0.5	-1.6	Subgiant	85
Hadai (β)	Centaurus	0.6	-5.1	Giant	460
Altair (α)	Aquila	0.8	2.2	Giant	16
Acrux (α)	Crux	0.8	-3.9	Subgiant	360
Betelgeuse (α)	Orion (var.)	0.8	-5.5	Supergiant	310
Aldebaran (α)	Taurus	0.9	-0.3	Giant	65
Spica (α)	Virgo	1.0	-3.5	Dwarf	260
Antares (α)	Scorpius (var.)	1.1	-4.5	Supergiant	330
Pollux (β)	Gemini	1.15	0.2	Giant	35
Fomalhaut (α)	Piscis Austrinus	1.2	2.0	Dwarf	420
Mimosa (β)	Crux	1.2	-5.0	Giant	570
Deneb (α)	Cygnus	1.3	-7.5	Supergiant	1800

STAR SIZES

Star sizes vary greatly. Dying white dwarf stars (page 47) are too small to be shown here. The Sun is much smaller than giant and supergiant stars like Antares and Betelgeuse, but these are huge because they have been puffed up by internal pressure. Their average density is about a thousandth of the air we breathe.

It is important to remember that star masses (the amount of material in them) do not vary by nearly as much as they do their diameters. Even a large star like Betelgeuse, whose volume is millions of times greater than the Sun's, has only about twenty times its mass.

Stars appear as pinpoints in any telescope, but in the case of the nearer and larger stars it is possible to 'process' their light and work out how large they must be. Betelgeuse has an average diameter greater than the orbits of Mars, mercury, Venus and the Earth. It was first measured in 1920.

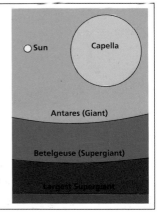

The Stars

Known as *proper motion*, this movement of the stars is the clue to likely neighbours. Even the largest proper motion, however, amounts to a shift equal to the Moon's width in 180 years, and most are only a tiny fraction of this.

Distances in the Sky

Distances between the stars are so great that remote Pluto seems only a step away. If the Sun is represented by a table-tennis ball, Pluto will be a speck of dust about 150 metres away, while the nearest star will be another ball about 1000 kilometres away. The compactness of the solar system is difficult to visualize.

The brightness of a star is no sure guide to distance, since star luminosities vary so much. But some nearby stars give a clue: measurements show that they are slowly changing their position with respect to the star patterns. All the stars in the Galaxy are shooting through space at speeds of many kilometres per second, and the nearer they are the more noticeable this motion becomes.

THE NEAREST STARS

Star		Constellation	Magnitude App	Abs.	Type	Distance (l.y.)	Proper motion ("/century)
Proxima		Centaurus	10.7	15.1	Dwarf	4.3	387
Rigel	A	Centaurus	0.0	4.4	Dwarf	4.3	367
Kent (α)	B	Centaurus	1.4	5.8	Dwarf	4.3	367
Barnard's star		Ophiuchus	9.5	13.2	Dwarf	5.2	1030
Wolf 359		Leo	13.5	16.7	Dwarf	7.6	467
Lalande 21185		Ursa Major	7.5	10.5	Dwarf	8.1	477
UV	A	Cetus	12.5	15.3	Dwarf	8.4	336
	B	Cetus	13.0	15.8	Dwarf	8.4	336
Sirius	A	Canis Major	-1.5	1.4	Dwarf	8.7	307
(α)	B	Canis Major	8.5	11.4	White dwarf	8.7	307
Ross 154		Sagittarius	10.6	13.3	Dwarf	9.5	74
Ross 248		Andromeda	12.2	14.7	Dwarf	10.3	182
ε		Eridanus	3.7	6.1	Dwarf	10.7	98
Ross 128		Virgo	11.1	13.5	Dwarf	10.8	136
61	A	Cygnus	5.2	7.5	Dwarf	11.1	520
	B	Cygnus	6.0	8.4	Dwarf	11.1	520
L789-6		Aquarius	12.2	14.6	Dwarf	11.2	327
ε		Indus	4.7	7.0	Dwarf	11.2	469
BD+4344	A	Andromeda	8.1	10.4	Dwarf	11.2	?
	B	Andromeda	11.1	13.4	Dwarf	11.2	?
Procyon (α)	A	Canis Minor	0.3	2.6	Sub-giant	11.4	125
	B	Canis Minor	10.8	13.1	White dwarf	11.4	125

The letters A and B refer to the brighter and fainter members of a binary star system (see page 50).

The Stars

▶ **Measuring a distance** by parallax. In the six months between the Earth moving from its January to its July position, stars A and B appear to shift against the distant background – the closer star B shifting more. Knowing the distance from the Earth to the Sun (the Astronomical Unit), each star's distance may be determined.

Earth based parallaxes can be used for distances of up to 100 light-years or so, but the Hipparcos astrometry satellite (1989-93) made accurate measurements for many more stars. Comparing a star's apparent and absolute magnitude also gives a key to its distance.

▼ **This diagram** shows the relative sizes of the Sun and its nearest companion star, as well as three planets and the Moon. To represent the relative distances, however, they would have to be separated by the amounts shown, and the whole Earth could only accommodate a few of the Sun's neighbours.

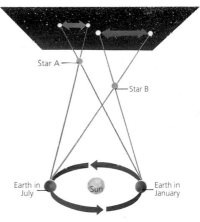

Star A

Star B

Earth in July

Sun

Earth in January

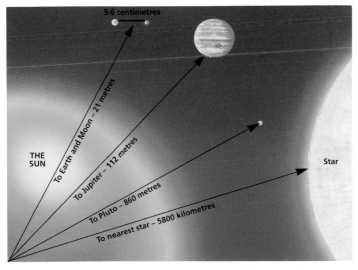

5·6 centimetres

THE SUN

To Earth and Moon – 21 metres

To Jupiter – 112 metres

To Pluto – 860 metres

To nearest star – 5800 kilometres

Star

The Stars

How the Stars Shine

Stars shine because of nuclear reactions deep in their interiors. They are made up mostly of hydrogen gas. The tremendous pressures in their centres raises the temperature to millions of degrees and in the heat the hydrogen atoms break down, recombining as helium. This releases enough energy to keep the process going as long as the hydrogen lasts.

But some stars are much hotter than others, and the colour of a star depends upon its temperature. White stars may have a surface temperature of 50,000°C; cool red stars may be below 3000°C. The Sun, at 5500°C, is yellowish.

A colour-magnitude (or Hertzsprung-Russell) diagram, shown opposite, plots surface temperature against absolute magnitude, and star families emerge. The most important is the *main sequence*, where most stars are found; they are known as *dwarfs*, to distinguish them from the inflated *giants* and *supergiants*. The *white dwarfs*, on the other hand, are small and dense, and are so dim that very few have been

discovered, although they almost certainly outnumber the giants.

The colour-magnitude diagram is rather like a photograph of a crowd of people – it shows the differences between individuals. It took astronomers a long time to realize how these various types of star are related. At first they thought that stars travelled along the main sequence. Current belief is that stars like the Sun originate to the right of the main sequence, spend most of their life at one point on it, inflate into the red giant domain, and then quickly cross it on their way to the white dwarf state at bottom left.

▶ HERTZSPRUNG-RUSSELL DIAGRAM
Bright stars are often given a special name of their own, such as Sirius. Others are known by a Greek letter, or a number, followed by the Latin genitive form of constellation name. In the diagram on the right, for example, we find ε Eridani (star ε in the constellation Eridanus) and 61 Cygni (star 61 in the constellation Cygnus). The Greek alphabet is given on page 50. A few unusual stars are named after the astronomer who examined them, such as Barnard's star.

THE STELLAR SPECTRUM

If starlight is passed through a spectroscope – a device to broaden it into a coloured band – a number of dark lines are usually seen. The coloured band is produced by the star's shining surface, while the dark lines indicate narrow strips of colour that have been absorbed by elements in it thin surrounding atmosphere.

By matching their lines with those obtained in a laboratory, astronomers can discover what elements are present in the star's atmosphere. However, the element helium was detected in the Sun before it was discovered on the Earth.

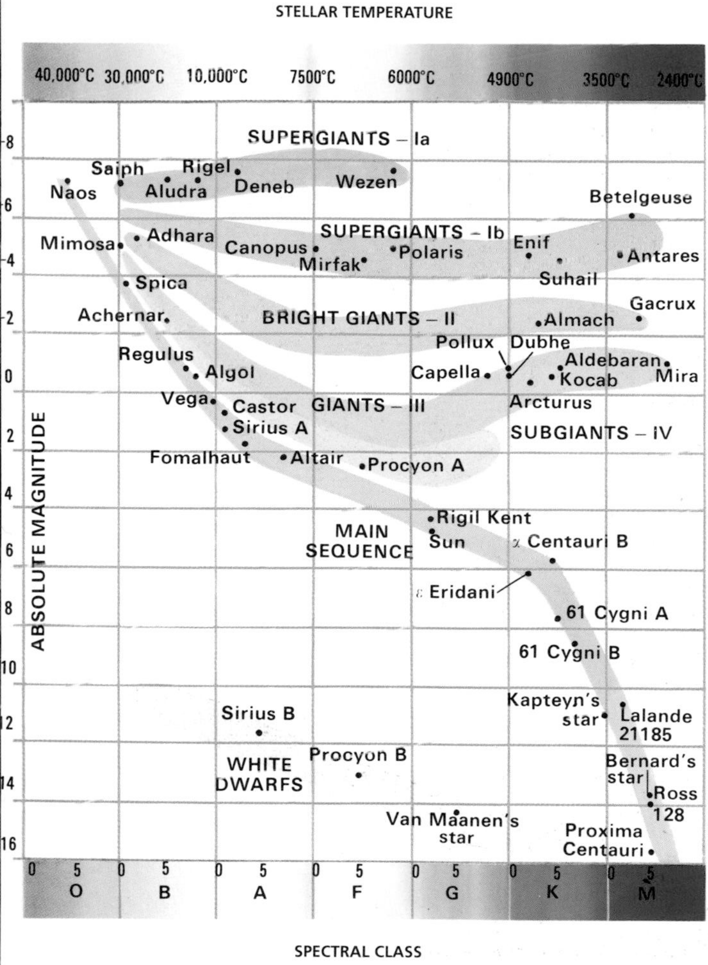

STELLAR TEMPERATURE

| 40,000°C | 30,000°C | 10,000°C | 7500°C | 6000°C | 4900°C | 3500°C | 2400°C |

SUPERGIANTS – Ia

Saiph   Rigel
Naos   Aludra   Deneb   Wezen
Betelgeuse

Mimosa   • Adhara   SUPERGIANTS – Ib   Enif
Canopus•   •Polaris   •Antares
Mirfak•   Suhail

• Spica   Gacrux
Achernar•   BRIGHT GIANTS – II   •Almach

Pollux   Dubhe
Regulus   Capella•   •Aldebaran•
•Algol   Kocab   Mira

Vega•   GIANTS – III   Arcturus
Castor
•Sirius A   SUBGIANTS – IV

Fomalhaut   •Altair   •Procyon A

•Rigil Kent
MAIN   Sun   α Centauri B
SEQUENCE

ε Eridani   • 61 Cygni A

61 Cygni B

Kapteyn's
Sirius B   star•   Lalande
•   21185

WHITE   Procyon B   Bernard's
DWARFS   •   star•
•Ross
128

Van Maanen's
star   Proxima
Centauri •

ABSOLUTE MAGNITUDE

| -8 | -6 | -4 | -2 | 0 | 2 | 4 | 6 | 8 | 10 | 12 | 14 | 16 |

| 0 | 5 | 0 | 5 | 0 | 5 | 0 | 5 | 0 | 5 | 0 | 5 | 0 | 5 |
| O | | B | | A | | F | | G | | K | | M | |

SPECTRAL CLASS

The Stars

The Life and Death of a Star

Stars form from the clouds of dust and gas called nebulae that make up a good proportion of the material in normal galaxies. When it becomes sufficiently dense, the nebula goes 'critical' and starts to condense into numerous clouds that are dark to begin with but heat up and begin to shine as stars. The temperature and brightness of the star depends upon the mass of the cloud.

Most stars, like the Sun, start life on the main sequence. But, as they burn their hydrogen, their cores become hotter and they emit shells of relatively cool gas: they have evolved into red giants like Aldebaran and Betelgeuse.

Eventually the shell disappears and only the intensely hot white core remains: the star is now a white dwarf, like Sirius B. A brilliant star like Deneb evolves in a few million years, whereas the much dimmer Sun will remain on the main sequence for thousands of millions of years.

▶ **A normal star** condenses from a dark cloud. it shines steadily for a long time, then expands into a red giant, and dies away as a tiny white dwarf. A very massive star may end its life in a supernova explosion.

▼ **The Sun** is an ordinary main-sequence star. Hydrogen atoms are turned into helium atoms in its searing core, releasing enormous amounts of energy.

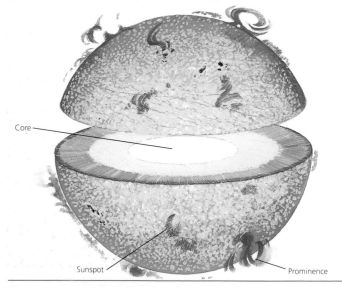

Core

Sunspot

Prominence

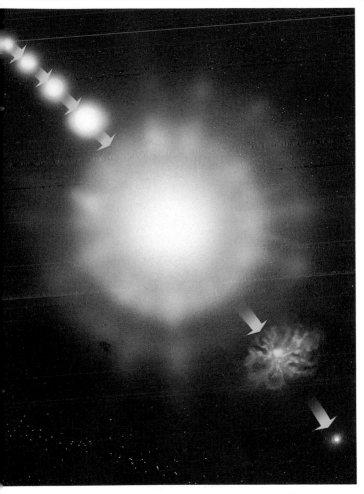

The Stars

Double Stars

If you look at star Zeta (ζ) in the constellation Ursa Major (Star Map 1, pp. 66-67), you will notice a much fainter star, Alcor, close to it. This is a naked-eye double star. Turn a small astronomical telescope on to the pair, and Zeta itself (usually known as Mizar) is seen to be a close double.

The Mizar-Alcor pair is known as an *optical* double; the stars are far apart, and just happen to be in almost the same direction. But Mizar is a true *binary*, and the stars are revolving around each other, although they may take about 14,000 years to complete a revolution.

The brighter star in a binary is known as the *primary*; the fainter as the *secondary*.

The distance between components of a double star is measured in seconds of arc ("). There are 60" in one minute of arc ('), and 60' equal one degree. An ordinary human hair, viewed from a distance of 12 metres, is about 1" thick. Good binoculars can separate normal double stars whose components are only 30" apart. The well-known double Beta Cygni (page 81) is an excellent test object for northern observers. If one star is much brighter than the other, its companion will be difficult to see because it may be hidden by the glare.

The table above lists examples of double stars, ranging from easy binocular objects to much closer pairs that will require a good telescope and high magnification to be seen.

WELL-KNOWN DOUBLE STARS

Constellation	Name	Magnitudes		Separation ("arc)
Andomeda	Gamma γ	2.3	5.1	9.8
Bootes	Epsilon ε	2.5	4.9	2.8
Cancer	Zeta ζ	5.1	6.2	6.0
Cassiopeia	Iota ι	4.6	6.9	2.5
Centaurius	Alpha α	0.0	1.3	14.1
Centaurus	Gamma γ	2.9	2.9	1.0
Crux	Alpha α	1.3	1.7	4.4
Cygnus	Beta β	3.1	5.1	34.4
Hercules	Zeta ζ	2.9	5.5	0.8
Leo	Gamma γ	2.2	3.5	4.4
Monoceros	Epsilon ε	4.5	6.5	13.4
Orion	Iota ι	1.9	4.0	2.3
Scorpius	Beta β	2.6	4.9	13.6
Ursa Major	Zeta ζ	2.3	4.0	14.4
Ursa Minor	Alpha α	2.0	9.0	18.4
Vela	Gamma γ	1.9	4.2	41.2
Virgo	Gamma γ	3.5	3.5	1.8

If the two stars are of different brightness, one eclipse is much deeper than the other (right). If they are similar, the eclipses resemble each other more closely (below right).

LETTERING THE STARS

The brighter stars in each constellation are given a Greek letter in approximately order of brightness, beginning with α. Since a number of these bright stars are important doubles, the Greek alphabet is given here:

α alpha	η eta	ν nu		t tau	
β beta	θ theta	ξ xi		υ upsilon	
γ gamma	ι iota	o omicron		φ phi	
δ delta	κ kappa	π pi		χ chi	
ε epsilon	λ lambda	ρ rho		ψ psi	
ζ zeta	μ mu	σ sigma		ω omega	

Eclipsing Binaries

In some binary systems the two stars are so close that no telescope can separate them. They can only be detected by double lines in the spectrum, or by one star eclipsing the other. The eclipse effect will be noticed only if the orbit appears almost edge-on as seen from the Earth.

Beta Persei (Algol) is an example of an *eclipsing binary*, consisting of a bright star and a dim star. In the diagram on the right, light from both stars reaches the Earth (1). After about 18 hours, (2), the dim star partly blocks off the bright star, and the total magnitude drops. At (3), one and a half days later, there is a slight brightness drop as the dim star is obstructed.

Another naked-eye eclipsing binary, Beta Lyrae, consists of two equal stars almost touching. The diagram below shows that its light change is continuous. These two binary systems represent the *dark-eclipsing* and *bright-eclipsing* families of variable stars and hundreds of members are known.

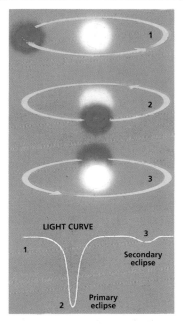

LIGHT CURVE

Secondary eclipse

Primary eclipse

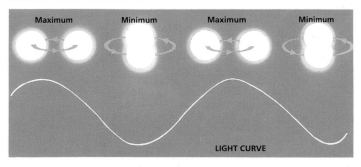

LIGHT CURVE

The Stars

Variable Stars

Eclipsing binaries are known as *extrinsic variables* since the stars themselves do not change in brightness. *Intrinsic variables* actually change in luminosity usually due to huge pulsations.

One well-known group is the *Cepheid* family, so called because the first one was discovered in the constellation Cepheus. These are yellow super-giant stars that brighten and fade by up to two magnitudes in a very regular manner. Cepheids are important, since their mean absolute magnitude is related to their period. By timing a Cepheid, its absolute magnitude can be determined. By comparing its absolute magnitude with its apparent magnitude, its distance can then be discovered.

Long-period variables (LPVs) form a very large group. They are red-giant stars with much longer periods than Cepheids. These range from about 200 to 500 days and vary by up to 10 magnitudes in brightness. They do not repeat themselves exactly from cycle to cycle. A famous long-period variable, Mira in Cetus, shows dramatic changes in its brightness; it has appeared almost as bright as the Pole Star, while at minimum it is only just visible with ordinary binoculars. Stars of this type are known as Mira stars.

▼ **Cepheid variables** repeat their brightness variations exactly from cycle to cycle, although some vary in brightness more than others. More luminous stars have longer periods.

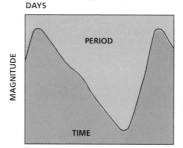

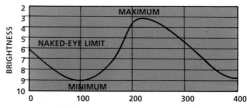

Observing Variable Stars

Variable-star observation is very popular with amateur astronomers. It consists of estimating the star's magnitude by comparing it with nearby *comparison stars* whose magnitude is known. There are several ways of making an estimate.

One way is to locate two comparisons, one brighter than the variable and the other fainter, and to decide how the variable 'fits' between them. It may be exactly midway in brightness, or closer to one or the other. With skill and experience, estimates can be accurate to 0·2 magnitude or even less. This is called the *fractional* method.

You can also try the *step* method, learning to recognize steps of 0·1 magnitude, and estimating by how many steps the variable differs from a comparison star.

Some advanced amateurs are now using electronic equipment to measure the brightness of variable stars. Accuracy of 0·01 magnitude is possible, but for many stars such precision is not necessary. For example, a family of stars known as dwarf novae spend most of their time at minimum brightness, but will suddenly rise by several tenths of a magnitude overnight. Other stars spend most of their time at maximum, and then plunge by several magnitudes in a few weeks.

This work is important, since professional astronomers cannot observe all the variable stars, and amateur-professional links are now well established. Variable star methods can also be used to estimate the brightness of small solar-system objects, such as comets and minor planets.

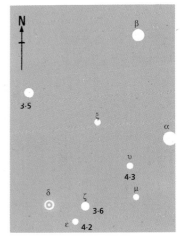

▲ **This chart** shows the brighter stars in Cepheus (page 79), with comparison stars for the famous variable δ (Delta).

◄ **This light-curve** of a long-period variable star (o Ceti, or Mira), shows how it rose and fell in brightness.

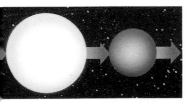

◄ **Mira stars** are a family of adolescent red giants, caught in a brief expanding and contracting phase as the star 'evolves' off the main sequence to become a red giant. Eventually the Sun may become a Mira star.

The Stars

Novae and Supernovae

Some variable stars are unpredictable and violent. Every few years a new naked-eye star suddenly shines out, literally overnight. This is a *nova*, a member of a close binary system which blasts off a huge shell of material. A nova can rise in brightness by over 10,000 times in a couple of days.

Some amateurs hunt for novae, scanning the Milky Way with binoculars. The most successful of this group G.E.D. Alcock of Peterborough, England, has found five since 1967. To discover a nova you must know the sky really well, so that a single extra star is readily spotted.

Supernovae are rarer still. This is the complete self-destruction of a massive star, and rivals an entire galaxy in brightness. In 1987 a supernova in the Greater Magellanic Cloud, a companion galaxy to our own Milky Way galaxy, could be seen with the naked eye. The previous nearby supernova occurred in 1604! All supernovae are shattered to pieces in their explosions, collapsing into neutron stars, smaller and denser than white dwarfs (see page 154).

VARIABLE STAR TYPES			
Star	**Magnitude range**	**Period**	**Map No**
Eclipsing binaries			
ε Aurigae	3.0 – 4.0	27.1 years	3
ζ Aurigae	3.8 – 4.3	972 days	3
β Lyrae	3.3 – 4.2	12.9 days	7
β Persei (Algol)	2.2 – 3.2	69 hours	3
Cepheid variables			
η Aquilae	4.1 – 5.4	7.2 days	7
δ Cephei	3.5 – 4.3	5.4 days	1
β Doradus	3.8 – 4.8	9.8 days	8
Long-period variables			
o Ceti (Mira)	3 – 10	330 days	2
χ Cygni	4 – 14	406 days	7
Irregular variables			
ρ Cassiopeiae	4 – 6	–	1
μ Cephei	4 – 5	–	1
α Herculis (Rasalgethi)	3 – 4	–	6
α Orionis (Betelgeuse)	0.4 – 1.3	5 years?	3
α Scorpii (Antares)	0.9 – 1.8	5 years?	6
Other variables			
γ Cassiopeiae	1.7 – 2.4	(Usually faint)	1
T Coronae Borealis	2 – 10	(Usually faint)	6
R Coronae Borealis	6 – 14	(Usually bright)	6

▲ **The Crab Nebula** is the remains of a supernova seen in 1054, equivalent in violence to a million million million million hydrogen bombs

▼ **The remnant of a supernova** thought to have occurred in 1657. This explosion involved a massive star weighing nearly 100 times more than the Sun.

Nebulae and Star Clusters

The word *nebula* means a cloud, and there are many cloudy-looking objects in the sky. But any comparison with terrestrial clouds is misleading. A cubic metre of rain cloud weighs perhaps 100 grammes, but a volume of nebula the size of the Earth would weigh only a few kilogrammes! Nebulae are noticeable only because they are so huge.

A nebula, like almost everything in the universe, consists mostly of hydrogen, although compounds of hydrogen with nitrogen, carbon, oxygen and other elements may be found. There are four main kinds of nebula:

Planetary nebulae are shells of gas expelled from very hot stars. They are called planetary nebulae because some

The Ring Nebula (below) was expelled from a star. The Horsehead (above) and Orion Nebula (left) indicate where young stars are forming.

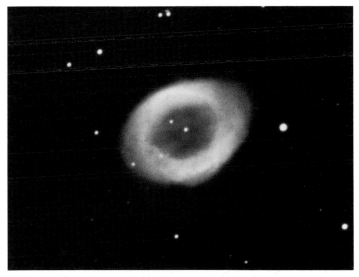

Nebulae and Star Clusters

of them appear disc-like in small telescopes. They are usually relatively small – less than a light-year across. Most are very faint. An example is M57 in Lyra (Star Map 7).

Reflection nebulae shine by reflected starlight, and are usually faint. An example is the Pleiades in Taurus (Star Map 3).

Emission nebulae are huge irregular clouds tens of light-years across. Within them stars are forming. They shine because their atoms react with radiation from nearby hot stars. An example is M8 in Sagittarius (Star Map 7).

Dark nebulae can be detected only by what they obscure. The Milky Way outline is irregular because of dark nebulae in front of the stars. An example is M42 in Orion (Star Map 3).

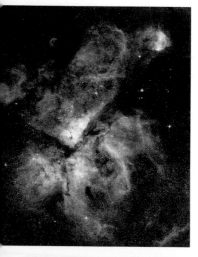

Star Clusters

Stars form in clusters rather than as individuals, condensing out of separate clouds within a nebula many light-years across. The Sun, presumably, was once a cluster member. But every star has a separate motion of its own, and unless the cluster is very compact so that the gravitational pull of its members holds the group together, the stars float apart over many millions of years.

These *open* clusters are being born all the time. For example, young stars are being formed in the Orion Nebula, M42. Clusters are very interesting to astronomers, since the stars in them form a mixed group of types, all of the same age. About 300 open clusters have been discovered in the Galaxy.

A cluster's likely age can be determined by examining its population. If it contains many very hot stars, it must be young – since such stars burn out quickly, or evolve into red giants. If it contains red giants and white dwarfs, it must be old.

Open clusters occur throughout the arms of the Galaxy, but *globular* clusters are completely different. They are about as old as the Galaxy itself, and contain red-giant stars. They measure up to 100 light-years across, and their population

◄ **The Keyhole Nebula** is at this moment giving birth to a cluster of stars.

► **The Pleiades** are a young cluster, probably less than 100 million years old. The six or seven brightest stars are detectable with the naked eye: they are white giant stars thousands of times as luminous as the Sun. They have not yet had time to evolve. As yet, there are neither red giants nor white dwarfs in the Pleiades.

Nebulae and Star Clusters

is reckoned in hundreds of thousands of stars. There are over 100 globular clusters in the Galaxy and many more in some other galaxies. They form a 'halo' around our star system.

Observing Star Clusters

The brightest open and globular clusters can be seen with the naked eye, provided the sky is really dark. Binoculars will give a good view of some of the larger open clusters. With apertures of from 60 millimetres to 150 millimetres, many are superb. Even experienced amateurs never tire of these objects.

You should remember that photographs taken with large telescopes show far more detail in clusters and nebulae than may be visible to the naked eye, even when using a large instrument. On the other hand, no photograph can capture the telescopic brilliance of stars sparkling in the eyepiece.

▲ **The Coal Sack** nebula obscures stars in the Milky Way.

▼ **Omega Centauri**, the finest globular cluster in the sky, lies well south of the celestial equator. It is easily visible with the naked eye.

The Constellations

The constellations are imaginary groupings of the stars. Invented years ago by people to help map the sky, they are still the easiest way to learn the stars. This chapter describes the most interesting of the 88 constellations, all of which are shown on the maps. Their brighter or more important stars are identified by name or letter. The standard three-letter abbreviation of each constellation is also given with each entry.

The stars are roughly grouped according to brightness, the largest circles representing the brightest stars. With care to keep out of all direct lights, the faintest stars shown here should be visible with the naked eye from suburban sites.

Nebulae and clusters, as well as galaxies, are given an 'M' number from Messier's 1781 catalogue (for example, the Orion Nebula, M42), or a number alone from the New General Catalogue (NGC) of 1888 (for example, the Double Cluster in Perseus, 869 and 884).

The Constellations

USING THE STAR MAPS

The maps on pages 66-75 represent the whole celestial sphere divided into six segments and the northern and southern circumpolar regions as shown below. The areas covered by each map, allowing for some overlap in RA, are as follows:

1 Dec +50° to N pole
2 RA 22h– 2h
3 RA 2h– 6h
4 RA 6h–10h   } Dec +50°
5 RA 10h–14h   to –50°
6 RA 14h–18h
7 RA 18h–22h
8 Dec –50° to S pole

The maps show all the stars in the sky down to about magnitude 4 5 as well as the positions of clusters, nebulae, and so on, usually known as 'deep-sky objects'.

These deep-sky objects are usually much fainter than the stars shown on the maps. Some special charts, to help locate the more difficult objects, have been added to the constellation notes.

There are also special charts for variable stars, which give the magnitudes of suitable comparison stars.

The light blue strip shows the path of the Milky Way and some of the more obvious irregularities in its course.

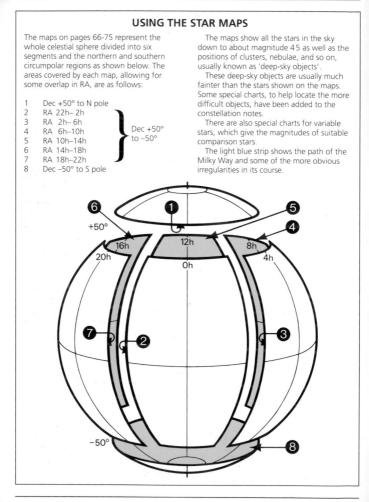

Finding a Star

Star maps can at first be very confusing.
It is difficult to compare the stars shown
flat on paper to the arc of stars in the sky
above. A good way of avoiding
disappointment is to learn to look for
some of the brighter stars. Once you are
familiar with these, the other patterns
will be easier to find.

The constellations Ursa Major and
Orion are so well known that they can be
used to identify other stars and groups.
Ursa Major is always in the northern
part of the sky, and is circumpolar for
much of Europe and the USA. Orion lies
on the celestial equator and is visible
everywhere in the world between
September and April. The region of Ursa
Major is shown on Star Maps 1 (pages
66-67) and 5 (page 71), while Orion
appears on Map 3 (page 69).

The diagrams on this page show
how to use different star alignments in
these two constellations. A more
systematic method is described below.

URSA MAJOR

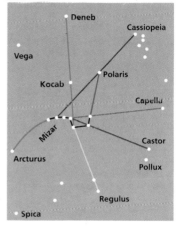

ORION

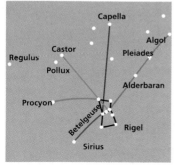

Where to look

All celestial objects are highest when
crossing the *meridian* (the north-south
line that passes overhead). Unless the
object is near the celestial pole, it will be
due south to a northern observer, and
due north to a southern one.

Take the Dec of the brightest star in
the constellation from the notes that
follow the star maps. Also find out the
co-latitude of your site (the co-latitude is
equal to 90 degrees (°) minus your
latitude.

Add the star's Dec to this amount,
and the result is the star's altitude above
the horizon as it crosses the meridian.
This is the angle to which you must set
your alidade.

Don't forget that if the star has a

The Constellations

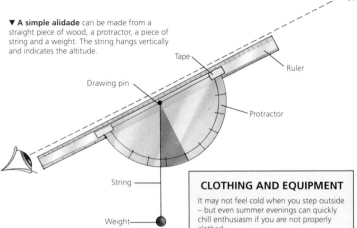

Star

▼ **A simple alidade** can be made from a straight piece of wood, a protractor, a piece of string and a weight. The string hangs vertically and indicates the altitude.

Tape

Ruler

Drawing pin

Protractor

String

Weight

southern Dec, you subtract the number from the complement. If you live south of the Equator, call south Dec positive and north Dec negative and add and subtract accordingly.

Timing Observations
As well as knowing *where* to look, you must know *when* to look. As the Earth turns, objects are carried past the meridian. The Sidereal Time (ST) gives the RA that is on the meridian at any moment.

For example, Regulus (Alpha Leonis) is at RA 10h 06m, so it is on the meridian just after 10h ST. To convert ST to GMT, for an observer standing on the Greenwich meridian, use the converter opposite. For example, if you are observing on January 31, 10h 06m

CLOTHING AND EQUIPMENT

It may not feel cold when you step outside – but even summer evenings can quickly chill enthusiasm if you are not properly clothed.

Good dark-adaptation is also essential. The eyes take at least ten minutes to acclimatize, so make sure that you have not left anything vital in a brightly-lit room.

Work with a dim red light. A bicycle rear lamp may be rather too bright. Try painting the bulk of an ordinary torch with red poster paint.

ST is about the same as 01h 30m GMT, or 1.30 am, so Regulus is on the meridian at this time. (Note that while GMT is used in the UK, observers in other parts of the world use their own local time system.) A better time to observe Leo would be in March; on March 31, for example, Regulus will be on the meridian at 21.30 GMT (9.30 pm).

Once you have identified a few of the brighter groups, the fainter constellations can be fitted into the gaps quite easily, using the maps in this book. Do not be content with learning just the brighter stars. Take a constellation and study it, using an atlas such as *Norton's Star Atlas* (see page 172), until you know the letters of all the naked-eye stars. If it is a Milky Way constellation, keep an eye out for a nova.

Very few amateurs have ever bothered to learn more than about 20 bright 'signpost' stars. But if you make an effort and observe systematically, you can memorize hundreds of stars.

Finally, buy a notebook and record all you learn and see (or fail to see!). You will come to treasure it later, and some of the information may be valuable in years to come. Include the date and time with all observations.

▼ **Use this diagram** to determine when a star of known RA will be on the meridian (GMT).

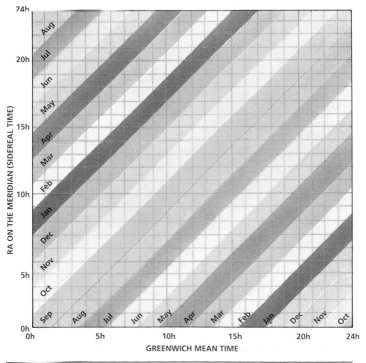

The Constellations

Star Map 1 – Northern Circumpolar Stars

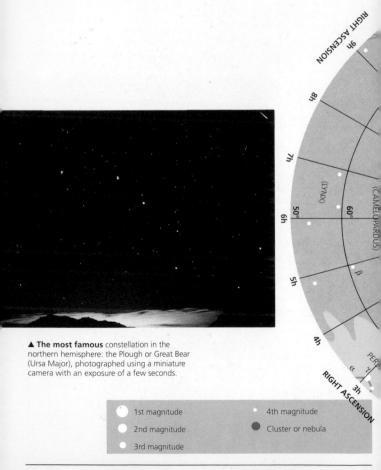

▲ **The most famous** constellation in the northern hemisphere: the Plough or Great Bear (Ursa Major), photographed using a miniature camera with an exposure of a few seconds.

RIGHT ASCENSION

9h

8h

7h

6h

5h

4h

3h

50°

60°

(LYNX)

(CAMELOPARDUS)

β

PER

α

RIGHT ASCENSION

○ 1st magnitude	· 4th magnitude
○ 2nd magnitude	● Cluster or nebula
○ 3rd magnitude	

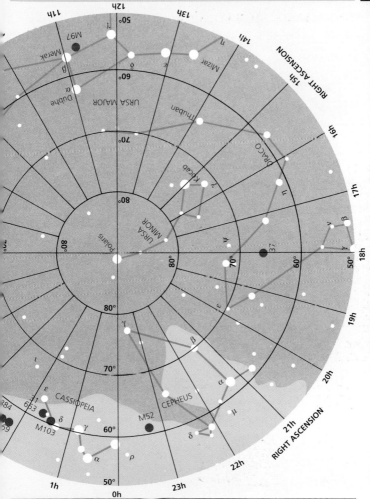

Star Map 2 – Right Ascension 22 Hours – 2 Hours

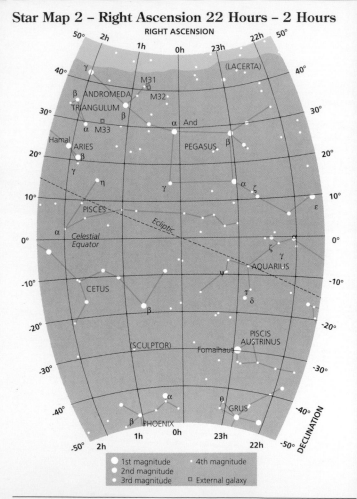

RIGHT ASCENSION

50° 2h 1h 0h 23h 22h 50°
40° γ (LACERTA) 40°
β ANDROMEDA M31 30°
TRIANGULUM M32
30° β
α M33 α And 30°
Hamal ARIES PEGASUS β 20°
20° β
γ
η γ α ζ
10° PISCES Ecliptic ε 10°
α Celestial Equator ζ γ α
0° AQUARIUS 0°
ψ
-10° CETUS τ δ -10°
β
-20° PISCIS -20°
(SCULPTOR) AUSTRINUS
Fomalhaut
-30° -30°
-40° α θ GRUS -40°
β PHOENIX DECLINATION
-50° 2h 1h 0h 23h 22h -50°

○ 1st magnitude · 4th magnitude
○ 2nd magnitude
○ 3rd magnitude □ External galaxy

Star Map 3 – Right Ascension 2 Hours – 6 Hours

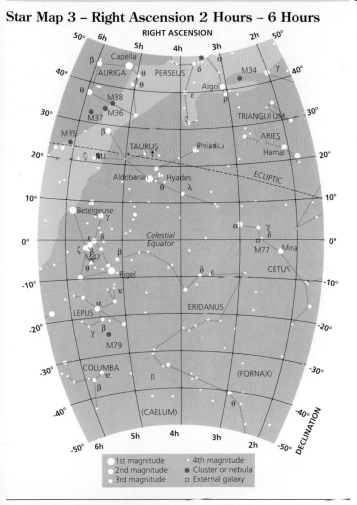

RIGHT ASCENSION

AURIGA
PERSEUS
Capella
β
θ
θ
θ
M38
M36
M37
M35
β
ζ
N11
TAURUS
Aldebaran
Hyades
θ
λ
Betelgeuse
γ
ε
δ
ζ
M42
θ
β
Rigel
κ
LEPUS
α
γ
β
M79
COLUMBA
α
β
(CAELUM)

δ
α
Algol
ε
ρ
ζ
M34
γ
TRIANGULUM
ARIES
Pleiades
Hamal
ECLIPTIC
Celestial
Equator
α
γ
δ
M77
Mira
CETUS
δ
ε
ERIDANUS
(FORNAX)
R
θ
(CAELUM)

DECLINATION

○	1st magnitude	○	4th magnitude
○	2nd magnitude	●	Cluster or nebula
○	3rd magnitude	▫	External galaxy

The Constellations

Star Map 4 – Right Ascension 6 Hours – 10 Hours

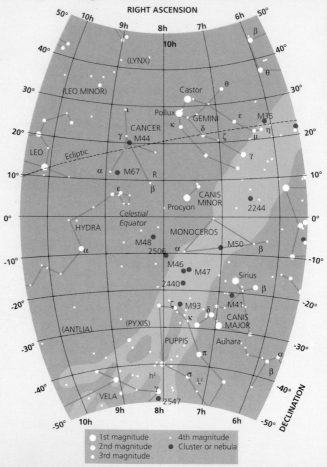

Star Map 5 – Right Ascension 10 Hours – 14 Hours

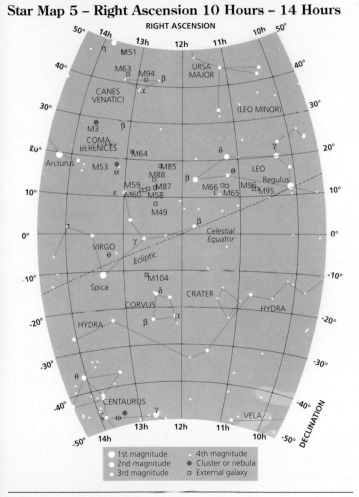

RIGHT ASCENSION

Key:
- ○ 1st magnitude
- ○ 2nd magnitude
- ○ 3rd magnitude
- • 4th magnitude
- ● Cluster or nebula
- □ External galaxy

The Constellations

Star Map 6 – Right Ascension 14 Hours – 18 Hours

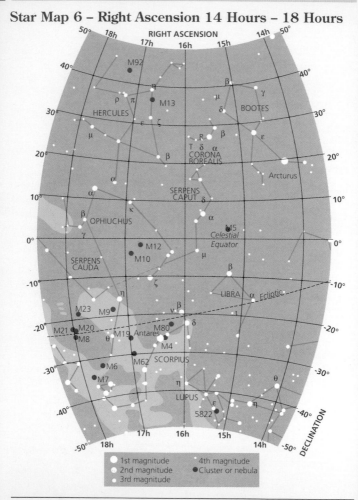

RIGHT ASCENSION

M92

HERCULES

ρ
π
η
M13
ε
ζ

μ

β

α

α
κ

β
OPHIUCHUS
γ

SERPENS
CAUDA

M12
M10

η
ζ

M23   M9

M21   M20
M8   θ   M19   Antares
M80
δ
M4
M62
M6   SCORPIUS
M7   η

LUPUS
ε
5822

BOOTES
β   γ
μ
δ

R
β
T δ α
CORONA
BOREALIS

SERPENS
CAPUT   δ

α
M5
Celestial
Equator

μ

β

LIBRA   α   Ecliptic
ι
ν β

θ

η

ε   η

Arcturus

DECLINATION

50° 40° 30° 20° 10° 0° -10° -20° -30° -40° -50°

18h 17h 16h 15h 14h

1st magnitude   **4th magnitude**
2nd magnitude   **Cluster or nebula**
3rd magnitude

72

Star Map 7 – Right Ascension 18 Hours – 22 Hours

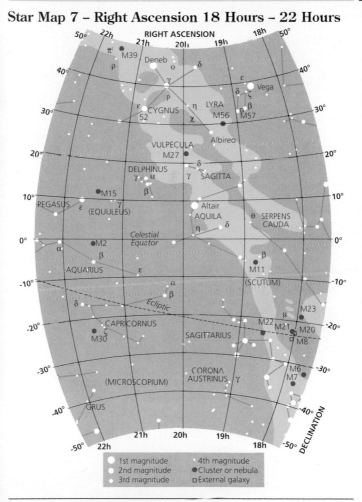

RIGHT ASCENSION

1st magnitude
2nd magnitude
3rd magnitude
4th magnitude
Cluster or nebula
External galaxy

The Constellations

Star Map 8 – Southern Circumpolar Stars

RIGHT ASCENSION

15h

16h

17h

18h

19h

20h

21h

(NORMA)

ARA

β

-50°

-60°

α

RIGHT ASCENSION

▲ **The Milky Way,** a fabulous sight among the circumpolar stars.

- ⚪ 1st magnitude
- ⚪ 2nd magnitude
- ⚪ 3rd magnitude
- · 4th magnitude
- 🔴 Cluster or nebula

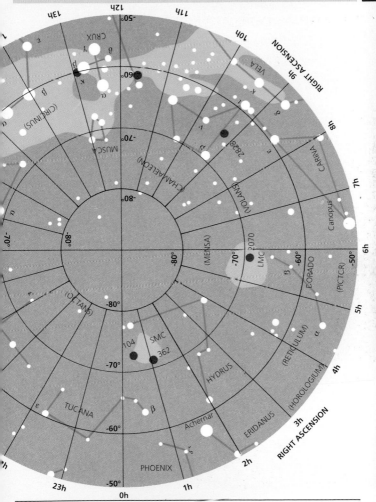

The Constellations

Observation Notes on the Constellations

All the stars and other objects mentioned in these notes can be found on the Star Maps and should be visible with binoculars, although the nebulae and clusters will look much more impressive if a powerful telescope is available.

Andromeda (And, Star Map 2)
This large constellation contains the famous Andromeda Galaxy, M31, easily seen with the naked eye in a dark sky; binoculars show a small hazy companion M32, both about two million light-years away. α (Alpheratz): RA 006h 06m, Dec +29°, mag 2.0.

▼ **The globular cluster** M2 in Aquarius is one of the most remote objects in the Galaxy visible with binoculars.

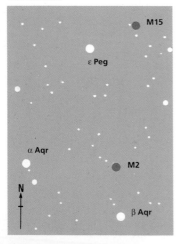

Apus, the Bird of Paradise
(Aps, Star Map 8)
A very faint group near the south pole. α: RA 14h 42m, Dec -79°, mag 3.8.

Aquarius, the Water Bearer
(Aqr, Star Maps 2 and 7)
This zodiacal constellation contains only two bright stars, but the little group of faint stars around ζ has a distinctive shape. Use the special chart to locate the globular cluster M2, which appears in binoculars as a very small hazy spot (diameter about 100 light-years; distance 55,000 light-years). The mag 4 star τ is a wide binocular double. α (Sadalmelik): RA 22h 03m, Dec –⅟₂°, mag 2.9 – one of the closest bright stars to the celestial equator.

Aquila, the Eagle (Aql, Star Map 7)
A notable Milky Way group whose brightest star, Altair, is one of the Sun's nearest neighbours, only 16 light-years away. η Aql is a bright Cepheid (see page 52); fine star fields near δ. α (Altair): RA 19h 48m, Dec +8⅟₂°, mag 0.8.

Ara, the Altar (Ara, Star Map 8)
A conspicuous, compact group in the southern Milky Way. β: RA 17h 21m, Dec –55⅟₂°, mag 2.8.

Aries, the Ram
(Ari, Star Map 3)
A small and rather faint group, but noticeable because there are few stars nearby. α (Hamal): RA 2h 04m, Dec +23°, mag 2.0.

▲ **An amateur** photograph of Auriga, showing the stars as trails. The brightest star is Capella.

Auriga, the Charioteer
(Aur, Star Map 3)

This is a magnificent constellation lying in a rather faint part of the northern Milky Way. Its three prominent open clusters, M36, M37 and M38, are all fine binocular objects, M37 being the largest. Theta is a challenging object for a 100-millimetre telescope (mags 2.6 and 7.1, separated by only 3.6″). ε is a very unusual dark-eclipsing variable star (see page 51) with a period of 27 years; the next minimum will occur in the year 2010! α (Capella): RA 5h 13m; Dec +46°, mag 0.1.

Boötes, the Herdsman
(Boo, Star Map 6)

A prominent kite-shaped group, with the brilliant reddish Arcturus in its 'tail'. δ has a mag 9 companion almost 2′ to the east, but there are few deep-sky objects. α (Arcturus): RA 14h 13m, Dec +19½°, mag –0.1.

Cancer, the Crab
(Cnc, Star Map 4)

A faint zodiacal group, interesting for the bright cluster Praesepe (M44), which looks like a large hazy patch with the naked eye. M44 must be much older than the Pleiades in Taurus because it contains no luminous white stars; they are all yellowish main-sequence dwarfs, or red giants. This group is about 15 light-years across and 500 light-years away. M67 is even older, and appears in binoculars as a misty spot. β: RA 8h 14m, Dec +9½°, mag 3.5.

Canis Major, the Greater Dog
(CMa, Star Map 4)

A brilliant Milky Way group, containing the brightest star in the sky, Sirius. Viewed from north European latitudes, Sirius never rises very high above the southern horizon, usually twinkling violently through the unsteady atmosphere. The open cluster M41 is easy to locate with binoculars. α (Sirius): RA 6h 43m, Dec –16½°, mag –1.5.

Canis Minor, the Lesser Dog
(CMi, Star Map 4)

Only its leading star is obvious; like Sirius, it is a binary with a white dwarf companion. α (Procyon): RA 7h 37m, Dec +5½°, mag 0.3.

The Constellations

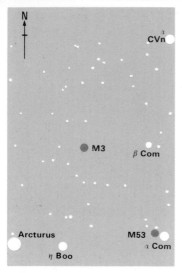

N

CVn
α

M3

β Com

Arcturus

M53
α Com

η Boo

▲ **M3**, in Canes Venatici, is one of the finest globular clusters in the sky, and appears in binoculars as a hazy patch on a line from α VCn towards Arcturus in Boötes.

Canes Venatici, the Hunting Dogs
(CVn, Star Map 5)
Only the leading star is obvious, lying south of Ursa Major. Use the accompanying chart to locate M3, one of the finest globular clusters. The external galaxy M51 may also be glimpsed as a very faint hazy disc. α (Cor Caroli): RA 12h 54m, Dec +38½°, mag 2·8.

Capricornus, the Sea Goat
(Cap, Star Map 7)
A large but faint zodiacal constellation, containing the wide naked-eye double star α (mags 3·6 and 4·3, 6′ 16″ apart), and an easy binocular double, β, which has a mag 6 companion 3′ 25″ away. The globular cluster M30 is a difficult binocular object from high northern latitudes. α (Dabih): RA 20h 18m, Dec −15°, mag 3·0.

Carina, the Keel (Car Star Map 8)
A large and brilliant southern constellation containing several bright clusters and groups, including the globular cluster NGC 2808, visible with binoculars. Magnificent sweeping in the Milky Way near Vela, α (Canopus): RA 6h 23m, Dec −52½°, mag −0·7.

Cassiopeia (Cas, Star Map 1)
A small but unmistakable constellation, its five brightest stars forming a conspicuous M or W near the north celestial pole. γ is an unusual variable, which suddenly brightened to mag 1·7 from its usual 2·4 in 1938. ρ, usually mag 5, sometimes fades to 6. There are rich Milky Way fields; note the clusters M52 and NGC 663 particularly. α (Shedir): RA 0h 38m, Dec +56½°, mag 2·2.

Centaurus, the Centaur
(Cen, Star Maps 5, 6 and 8)
An extensive constellation. α is a magnificent binary star although it cannot be resolved without a proper telescope. Known as Rigel Kent, it is the closest naked-eye star to the Sun. Centaurus contains the closest and brightest globular cluster in the sky, labelled ω. Binoculars show it as an immense hazy patch about two-thirds the Moon's diameter. α (Rigel Kent): RA 14h 36m, Dec -60½°, mag 0·1.

▲ **This 1-minute** exposure with a fixed camera shows Cassiopeia, part of Perseus, and the Double Cluster between them.

Cepheus (Cep, Star Map 1)
Not easy to identify, but contains interesting objects. μ was called the Garnet Star by Herschel because of its port-wine colour; it is slightly variable. δ is the prototype Cepheid (see page 53 and use the chart given there to observe its changes). It has a mag 5 companion 41″ away. α (Alderamin): RA 21h 17m Dec +62½°, mag 2·4.

Cetus, the Whale
(Cet, Star Maps 2 and 3)
An extensive faint constellation, although the little triangle of α, γ and δ is fairly obvious. Mira, or o, is a long-period variable mentioned on page 52, ranging from about mag 10 at minimum to a bright as mag 2 (but usually about

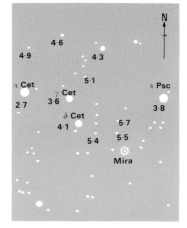

▲ **If the long-period** variable Mira (o Ceti) is above magnitude 6, it can be located with this chart and followed as it brightens or fades.

The Constellations

mag 4) at maximum, in a period of about 11 months. The next observable maxima should occur at the beginning of March 1996 and the end of January 1997, in the evening sky. α (Menkar): RA 3h 00m, Dec +4½°, mag 2·7.

Coma Berenices, Berenices' Hair
(Com, Star Map 5)

Although containing no star brighter than mag 4, Coma can be distinguished as a faint scattering of stars in an otherwise dull patch of sky. It contains one of the largest clusters of galaxies known – several thousand of them – but only a few are prominent. The chart shows the positions of two that are just visible with binoculars (M64 and M85); M53 is brighter than either, but is a globular cluster. Both galaxies are about 40 million light-years away. α RA 13h 08m, Dec +18°, mag 4·2.

The adjacent regions of Leo and Virgo also contain numerous galaxies, and these are all part of the Local Supercluster, which spreads across 100 million light-years of space.

▼ **Some of the brighter** galaxies in the Coma-Virgo region, together with the globular cluster M53, the easiest Messier object shown here.

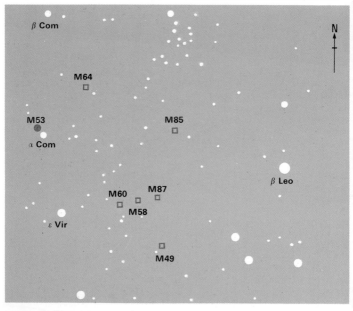

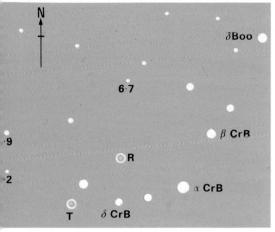

N

6·7

δ**Boo**

β **CrB**

·9

R

·2

α **CrB**

T   δ **CrB**

◄ **A chart** for the unusual variables R and T Coronae Borealis.

Corona Borealis, the Northern Crown (CrB, Star Map 6)
Although small, this group is easily identified from its semi-circular outline. Note variable R, normally mag 6, which at unpredictable intervals sinks in a few days to as faint as mag 14; see the chart above. T rose to brief naked-eye visibility in 1866 and 1946. α (Alphecca): RA 15h 33m, Dec +27°, mag 2.3.

Crux, the Cross (Crx, Star Map 8)
The smallest constellation in the sky, but one of the most famous. It contains one of the finest double stars, α,(Acrux), mags 1·4 and 1·9, separation 4·4″. Its position is RA 12h 24m, Dec −63°.

Cygnus, the Swan (Cyg, Star Map 7)
One of the finest northern constellations, the Milky Way about γ being particularly rich. It contains the bright cluster M39, but the stars are too scattered for the best effect. o is one of the finest binocular pairs, the mag 4 yellow star making the mag 5 companion look blue. β (mags 3 and 5·5, separation 34″) may just be divided. Note also the long-period variable χ, which at maximum reaches mag 4·5, and can be identified by its reddish colour. Its period is about 406 days. α (Deneb): RA 20h 40m, Dec +45°, mag 13.

Delphinus, the Dolphin
(Del, Star Map 7)
A small but distinct constellation near a bright section of the Milky Way. In 1967, a naked-eye nova was discovered within its boundaries. γ is a beautiful double, mags 4 and 5, separation 10″. RA 20h 38m, Dec +15°, mag 38.

The Constellations

Dorado, the Dolphin
(Dor, Star Map 8)
A far southern constellation, interesting mainly because it contains one of the Galaxy's satellites, the Large Magellanic Cloud, about 160,000 light-years away and looking like a large hazy patch. This contains many superb objects including NGC 2070, a naked-eye emission nebula. β is a bright Cepheid (see page 52). α: RA 4h 33m, Dec −55°, mag 3·3.

Draco, the Dragon (Dra, Star Map 1)
This is a winding constellation extending around a large arc of the northern sky. The two stars β and γ are the easiest to identify. Nearby is ν, a very attractive pair of mag 5 stars about 1′ apart, α (Thuban): RA 14h 03m, Dec +64½°, mag 3·6.

Equuleus, the Little Horse
(Equ, Star Map 7)
This tiny constellation contains only three obvious stars. One of them, γ, is an attractive wide double, mags 4·5 and 6. α: RA 21h 13m, Dec +5°, mag 3·9.

Eridanus (Eri, Star Maps 3 and 8)
A winding constellation extending from the far southern sky to equatorial latitudes. Note the reddish tint of γ, a red giant star. α (Achernar): RA 1h 36m, Dec −57½°, mag 0·5.

Gemini, the Twins (Gem, Star Map 4)
One of the most interesting of all constellations. It lies on the most northern part of the ecliptic, and the Sun moves into it from adjacent Taurus on the first day of northern summer. At this time it is only a degree or so away from

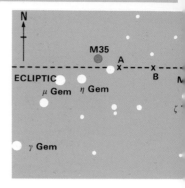

▲ **In Gemini,** A is the Sun's position at northern midsummer, B is where Uranus was found in 1781.

the bright open cluster M35. This is also the point where Herschel discovered the planet Uranus in 1781. μ and η both have lovely golden tints, while ε and ζ have faint binocular companions, the latter being the more impressive. β (Pollux): RA 7h 42m, Dec +28°, mag 1·1.

Hercules (Her , Star Map 6)
Not obvious until the quadrilateral or 'keystone' of π, η, ζ and ε is identified, but a fine constellation for the double-star enthusiast armed with an adequate telescope. M13 is its most famous object: one of the brightest globular clusters in the sky, and just visible with the naked eye. It is about 25,000 light-years away and may contain half a million stars. M92, another globular, is harder to find because there are no nearby bright stars as guides; it is half as far away again as M13, α (Rasalgethi): RA 17h 12m, Dec +14½°, mag 3·5 (slightly variable).

The Constellations

Hydra, the Water Serpent
(Hya, Star Maps 4 and 5)
A faint, rambling group; only Alphard and the little collection of stars south of Cancer, marking its head, are obvious. α (Alphard): RA 9h 25m Dec –8½°, mag 2·0.

Leo, the Lion (Leo, Star Map 5)
A zodiacal constellation, α lying within a degree of the ecliptic, so that both the Moon and the planets can occult it. Leo lies near the huge groups of galaxies in Coma and Virgo, and at least two objects, M65 and M66, are just detectable with binoculars if the sky is dark; use the accompanying chart to locate them. α (Regulus): RA 10h 06m, Dec +12°, Mag 1·4.

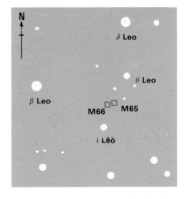

▲ **The pair** of spiral galaxies M65 and M66, in Leo.

Lepus, the Hare (Lep, Star Map 3)
A small but conspicuous group south of Orion. γ is a very fine binocular double (mags 4 and 6·5, separation 1½'), while the globular cluster M79 can be seen as a hazy spot. α (Arneb): RA 5h 31m, Dec –18°, mag 2·6.

Libra, the Scales (Lib, Star Map 6)
A large zodiacal constellation, but only α and β are obvious. α has a wide mag 6 companion. α (Zubenelgenubi): RA 14h 48m, Dec –16°, mag 2·8.

Lupus, the Wolf (Lup, Star Map 6)
A small but prominent constellation in a rich region of the southern Milky Way. η is a mag 4 star with a mag 9 companion 2' away, and NGC 5822 is a bright open cluster. α: RA 14h 39m, Dec –47°, mag 2·3.

◀ **Dense star-field** near γ Cygni.

The Constellations

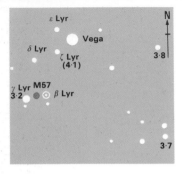

▲ **A chart** for the eclipsing star β Lyrae, also showing the position of M57, the Ring Nebula.

Lyra, the Lyre (Lyr, Star Map 7)

A small but most interesting group. ε can be separated by acute naked eyesight; ζ (mag 4) has a mag 6 companion 44′ away. δ is another naked-eye pair. β is an eclipsing binary (see page 51): it is almost as bright as its neighbour when at its brightest, but a magnitude dimmer when passing through an eclipse. M57, the famous Ring Nebula, is barely detectable with binoculars; M56 is a faint globular, α (Vega): RA 18h 35m, Dec +38½°, mag 0·0.

Monoceros, the Unicorn

(Mon, Star Map 4)
Most of the stars in this group are faint, but the Milky Way is magnificent. The cluster NGC 2244 can be seen with the naked eye. M50 and NGC 2506 are other fine clusters. M50 is so compact that it appears as a hazy patch when viewed with binoculars. α: RA 7h 39m, Dec −9½°, mag 3·9.

Ophiuchus, the Serpent Bearer
(Oph, Star Map 6)
Although not one of the twelve zodiacal constellations, the ecliptic passes through it. Superb Milky Way fields to the south; M10 and M12 are bright globular clusters, while M9, M19 and M62 are fainter globulars. The whole region is well worth sweeping on a clear night. An obvious binocular group of 8th magnitude stars about a degree away from β was not, strangely enough, included in the early catalogues of deep-sky objects. α (Rasalhague): RA 17h 33m, Dec +12½°, mag 2·1.

▼ **The constellation** Lyra with its bright star Vega.

The Constellations

Orion (Ori, Star Map 3)
This brilliant constellation contains no less than seven 1st magnitude stars – more than any other group. All, Betelgeuse apart, form a true association in space, being hot young stars. Rigel (β) is one of the most luminous known stars in the Galaxy, 50,000 times as bright as the Sun. δ is a difficult binocular double, with a mag 6·5 companion to the north 53″ away. The famous Great Nebula (M42) shows many irregularities due to dark nebulae. β (Rigel): RA 5h 12m Dec –8½°, mag 0·1.

Pavo, the Peacock (Pav, Star Map 8)
This group contains two interesting stars: κ, a Cepheid (mag 3·9 – 4·9, period 9·1 days), and λ, an irregular variable, mag range 3·5–4·5. NGC 6752 is a huge globular cluster, over half the Moon's diameter across. α: RA 20h 22m; Dec –57°, mag 1·9.

Pegasus (Peg, Star maps 2 and 7)
The Great Square is easy to recognize once located, but it is not always easy to find at first because it appears larger in the sky than on a map. ε is an easy binocular double (mags 2·5 and 8·5, separation almost 2′), and this acts as a guide to M15, a globular cluster easily seen in binoculars. α (Markab): RA 23h 02m, Dec +15°, mag 2·5.

Perseus (Per, Star Maps 1 and 3)
A magnificent constellation in the northern Milky Way. Its most famous object is the eclipsing binary β (Algol), described on page 51. NGC 869 and 884 form the Double Cluster, visible with the naked eye and a fine binocular object.

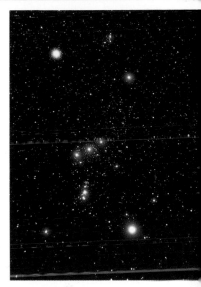

▲ **This photograph** shows the three 'belt' stars of Orion, with the Great Nebula, M42, to the south.

M34, a more scattered cluster, can also be seen with the naked eye. α (Mirfak): RA 3h 21m, Dec +50°, mag 1·8.

Pisces, the Fishes (Psc, Star Map 2)
A faint, straggling zodiacal group, containing the vernal equinox – the point where the Sun crosses the celestial equator at the beginning of northern spring. Due to the very slow gyration of the Earth's axis, the vernal equinox lay in the adjacent constellation of Aries two millennia ago. α (Katain): RA 1h 59m, Dec +, 2½°, mag 3·8.

The Constellations

▲ **The Double Cluster** in Perseus lies in a rich region of the Milky Way.

Piscis Austrinus, the Southern Fish
(PsA, Star Map 2)
A small group marked by its leader Fomalhaut, which shines in an empty part of the sky. α (Fomalhaut): RA 22h 55m, Dec –30°, mag 1·2.

Puppis, the Poop (Pup, Star Map 4)
This small bright group contains many open clusters and fine Milky Way fields. Note particularly M47, a magnificent loose group almost equal to the Moon's diameter, and M93. M46 is rather faint for binocular observation. ζ: RA 8h 02m, Dec –40°, mag 2·3.

Sagitta, the Arrow (Sge, Star Map 7)
A small but distinctive group lying in the Milky Way. Look just south of the midway point between γ and δ for M71 (see chart on page 90). Appearing as a dim hazy spot, it is either a very compressed open cluster or a very

unusual globular. γ: RA 19h 57m, Dec +19°, mag 3·5.

Sagittarius, the Archer
(Sgr, Star Map 7)
A superb zodiacal constellation lying in the densest part of the Milky Way – the region towards the centre of the Galaxy. Clusters and nebulae are strewn so thickly that no guide to interesting objects is really necessary, and the ones shown on the map are only a few of the more obvious. M8, the Lagoon Nebula, is a bright cluster enveloped in haze, while M20 is the Trifid Nebula, a prominent irregular patch next to the open cluster M21. M23 is another bright cluster, while M22 is a super globular. The constellation contains 15 Messier objects altogether, but most are poorly seen from high northern latitudes. ε (Kaus Australis): RA 18h 21m, Dec –34¹/₂°, mag 1·8.

Scorpius, the Scorpion
(Sco, Star Map 6)
After Orion, perhaps the most brilliant constellation in the sky, with red Antares in its head and a curved 'sting' behind. Like its neighbour Sagittarius, Scorpius contains the densest part of the Milky Way and clusters and nebulae abound, but there are also some interesting stars. Antares is a red supergiant as large as the orbit of Mars, and slightly variable. ν is an attractive binocular double, mags 4·5 and 6·5, separation 41″. M4 and M80 are both globular clusters, M4 being the

▶ **The Trifid Nebula** is about 2300 light-years away from the Sun. The lanes are due to huge dark interstellar clouds between us and the nebula.

larger of the two and lying in the same binocular field as Antares itself. The open clusters M6 and M7 are among the finest in the sky. α (Antares): RA 16h 26m, Dec $-26\frac{1}{2}°$, mag about 1·1 (variable).

Scutum, the Shield (Sct, Star Map 6)
A faint but distinctive group lying in a magnificent region of the Milky Way, containing the superb open cluster M11. α: RA 18h 32m, Dec $-8\frac{1}{2}°$, mag 3·8.

Serpens, the Serpent
(Ser, Star Map 6)
This constellation represents a snake being held by Ophiuchus, and is divided into head (Caput) and body (Cauda). It contains M5 (see chart on opposite page), one of the largest and brightest globular clusters. δ is a fine double star (mags 4·2 and 5·2, separation 4·4″) α (Unukalhai): RA 15h 42m, Dec $+6\frac{1}{2}°$, mag 2·7.

The Constellations

◀ **Red Antares** in Scorpius.is a giant star about 500 light-years away, it is about 10,000 times as luminous as the Sun.

Taurus, the Bull
(Tau, Star Map 3)

A prominent zodiacal group with more than its share of interesting objects. The bright, very scattered Hyades cluster, to the west of Aldebaran, looks in binoculars like a sprinkle of coloured jewels. The Pleiades, three times as distant at about 400 light-years, are much more compact, and contain very luminous white stars of a type that has burnt out and disappeared in the much older Hyades. At its distance of only 65 light-years, Aldebaran is twice as close as the Hyades. τ is an attractive binocular double, mags 4·5 and 8··5, distance 1'. The planetary M1 may just be spotted, about 1° NW of ζ; this is the Crab Nebula, the remains of the supernova of 1054, α (Aldebaran): RA 4h 33m, Dec + 16½°, mag 0·9.

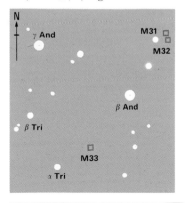

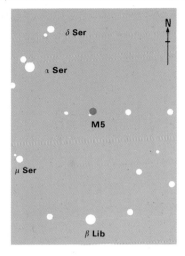

▲ **M5 in Serpens** rivals the Great Cluster in Hercules in brightness It is 27,000 light-years away from Earth.

Triangulum, the Triangle
(Tri, Star Map 2)

A small but fairly distinct group containing the interesting galaxy M33. At least as large as the Moon, it is excessively faint and difficult to see: a real challenge for the clearest of nights. Excellent dark adaptation is essential. Let the binoculars slowly pass over the suspect area and use averted vision, which means directing the gaze away from the region so that the image falls on the more sensitive margin of the retina. Only slightly further off than M31, it is a much smaller object, with

◀ **Elusive M33**, in Triangulum, can just be detected with binoculars in a transparent sky.

The Constellations

about 1/40th of its mass. β: RA 2h 07m, Dec +35°, mag 3·0.

Triangulum Australe, the Southern Triangle (TrA, Star Map 8)
A small high southern group on the edge of the Milky Way. NGC 6025 is a fine open cluster. α: RA 16h 43m, Dec -69°, mag 1·9.

Tucana, the Toucan (Tuc, Star Map 8)
Containing the small Magellanic Cloud, this constellation also includes the brilliant globular cluster 47 (NGC 104), which rivals ω Cen. β may be too difficult for binoculars: mags both 4·5, separation 27″. NGC 362 is another fine globular. α: RA 22h 15m, Dec −60½°, mag 2·8.

Ursa Major, the Great Bear (UMa, Star Maps 1 and 5)
Sometimes known as the Plough or the Dipper, the outline of this constellation is known to most people, although it extends far beyond the seven bright stars. ζ (Mizar) is mentioned on page 50. The faint planetary cluster M97 may be spotted with binoculars in a very dark sky. α (Dubhe): RA 11h 01m, Dec +62°, mag 1·8.

Ursa Minor, the Little Bear (UMi, Star Map 1)
The north polar constellation, containing the Pole Star or Polaris. α (Polaris): RA 02h 15m, Dec +89°, mag 2·0.

Vela, the Sails (Vel, Star Maps 4 and 8)
A bright Milky Way group. γ is a testing double (mags 1·8 and 4·2, distance 42″), just resolvable in good binoculars. The nearby cluster NGC 2547 can be seen

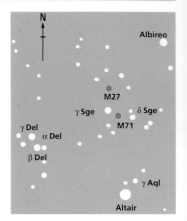

with the naked eye. γ: RA 8h 08m, Dec −47°, mag 1·7.

Virgo, the Virgin (Vir, Star Map 5)
A large zodiacal constellation, best known for the galaxies within its confines, though few are visible with binoculars. The chart on page 80 shows the positions of the brightest (M49, M58 and M87), as well as the fainter M60. α (Spica): RA 13h 23m, Dec −11°, mag 1·0.

Vulpecula, the Fox (Vul, Star Map 7)
This is a very small Milky Way group, but it contains M27, one of the largest and brightest planetary nebulae in the sky (see chart). α: RA 19h 27m, Dec +24½°, mag 4·4.

▶ **The large** planetary M27 the Dumb-bell nebula, is a bright binocular object, but is not easy to locate among the many faint stars in Vulpecula – see the chart (above). M71 in Sagitta is also shown.

The Moon

O f all the objects in the sky, the Moon is the one that appears to undergo the most dramatic change, since it passes through a complete cycle of phases once a month. This change, though, is only one of movement and light. The lunar surface is inert, airless and dead; the last dramatic events happened there some 3000 million years ago, and they are still recorded, apparently fresh, on its crater-pocked face.

The Moon passes through phases because it shines only by reflecting sunlight. The Moon, like the Earth, is always half-lit by the Sun. As it goes through its phases night by night, different features of its surface are illuminated. A considerable amount of detail can be seen with a small telescope or binoculars, so it is not surprising that the Moon is the favourite object for anyone taking up astronomy as a hobby.

The Moon's Cycle

It takes the Moon 29½ days to pass through its phases and this is known as the lunar month. During this time, the sunrise and sunset line, or *terminator*, slowly passes across the Earth-turned hemisphere: sunrise before Full, sunset after Full.

At New Moon, the dark hemisphere faces the Earth and cannot be seen, since it is very near the Sun in the sky. After two or three days, it has moved far

▼ **The Moon** shows phases because the Sun can illuminate only one hemisphere. It rotates once on its axis during the lunar month, therefore always keeping the same face towards the Earth.

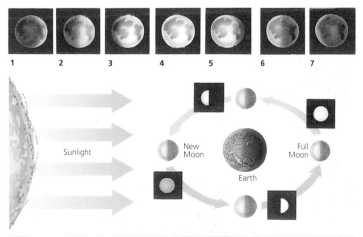

Sunlight

New Moon

Earth

Full Moon

The Moon

enough east to be seen as a thin crescent in the evening sky; after seven days it forms a perfect half, known as First Quarter, lying about 90 degrees away from the Sun.

The following week sees it in the *gibbous* state, until at Full it is situated opposite the Sun in the sky, rising at sunset. After this, the phases pass in the reverse order, the Moon rising later and later in the night, until it disappears in the dawn sky.

Unless the line-up between the three bodies is perfect and an eclipse occurs, the Moon is invisible at New since it is hidden in the Sun's glare. It is interesting to try to spot the thin crescent setting in the west a couple of days after New or rising in the east a couple of days before New. Binoculars will be a help in locating the hair-thin line of light, perhaps with the complete dark side also faintly illuminated by reflected light from the Earth.

MOON FACTS

Diameter:	3476 kilometres
Mass:	0.012 X Earth
Density:	3.3 X water
Mean distance:	384,400 kilometres
Minimum distance:	
	356,400 kilometres
Maximum distance:	
	406,700 kilometres
True (sidereal) period of rotation:	
	27.32 days
Phase cycle (synodic period):	
	29.53 days
Inclination of orbit to ecliptic:	5°
Axial inclination:	6½°
Angular diameter:	
	29′ 21″ (min.); 33′ 30″ (max.)

▲ **The Earth-turned** face of the Moon (top), has numerous lava plains or maria; the far side (below) is totally cratered.

◄ **The Moon** shows phases because the Sun can illuminate only one hemisphere. It rotates once on its axis during the lunar month, therefore always keeping the same face towards the Earth.

The Moon

Lunar Eclipses

If the Moon moved exactly along the ecliptic (which could happen only if it revolved exactly in the plane of the Earth's orbit), the line-up with the Sun at New and Full would be perfect and there would always be an eclipse of the Sun and the Moon respectively at these times.

However, the Moon's orbit is inclined at five degrees to the ecliptic, so eclipses are rather rare. A lunar eclipse occurs when the Moon passes into the Earth's shadow. At a total eclipse it passes completely into the central shadow or umbra. An eclipse may last for several hours and may be total for well over an hour. But even when it is totally eclipsed, the Moon is always dimly visible because the Earth's atmosphere passes some light into the shadow, giving it a reddish-brown colour.

▼ **An eclipse** of the Moon occurs when it passes through the long shadow cast by the Earth. An eclipse of the Moon occurs when it passes through the long shadow cast.

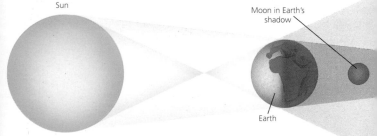

Sun

Moon in Earth's shadow

Earth

LUNAR ECLIPSES					
Date and Time (GMT) of mid-eclipse			Type	Duration (minutes)	Region of Visibility
1996	Apr	4	00.07	Total	84	Asia, Africa, Europe, USA
	Sep	27	02.51	Total	72	Europe, Africa, USA
1997	Mar	24	04.45	Partial	–	Africa, Europe, USA
	Sep	16	18.50	Total	66	Australia, Africa, Asia, Europe
1999	Jul	28	11.25	Partial	–	USA, Pacific, Australia
2000	Jan	21	04.40	Total	80	Asia, Africa, Europe, USA

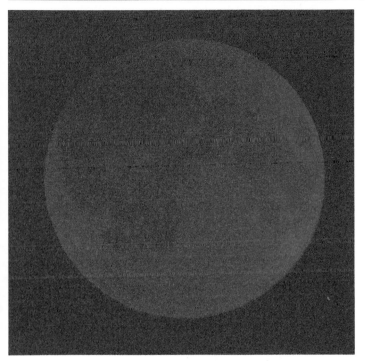

Total eclipses are particularly interesting, because some are much darker than others. This is due to the varying transparency of the atmosphere. Partial eclipses on the other hand are of little interest since the dazzling uneclipsed portion of the surface blots out the delicate shadow colouring. The eclipse of December 30, 1982, was so dark that the Moon could hardly be seen with the naked eye, but on most

▲ **Total eclipse of the moon** in the progress of a lunar eclipse. It can take up to six hours for the Moon to pass completely through the Earth's shadow, and the totality of the eclipse can last for 1¾ hours.

occasions the very bright and very dark features, such as maria and ray craters, are visible with binoculars.

Unlike solar eclipses, lunar eclipses look the same from everywhere the Moon is above the horizon.

The Moon

Occultations by the Moon

As the Moon (and a planet too, for that matter) passes along the ecliptic, it regularly moves in front of stars and blocks them from view. Such a phenomenon is called an *occultation*. Although occultations can be predicted for years in advance, there is always an uncertainty of a second or more in the exact instant at which the star vanishes or reappears.

Stars disappear at the eastern edge or limb, which before Full is invisible unless the Moon is a crescent and its dark side can be seen faintly illuminated by *Earthshine* – sunlight reflected on to it from the Earth. Dark-limb occultations are much easier to observe than bright-limb events, because the star is easily

▼ **By timing** the disappearance or reappearance of a star at an occultation, the Moon's position in its orbit can be accurately determined, since the star acts as a reference point in the sky.

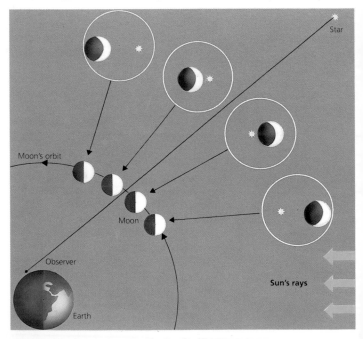

Star

Moon's orbit

Moon

Observer

Earth

Sun's rays

lost in the glare of the Moon. Planets are also occulted by the Moon and it can be very exciting to watch as the Moon gradually cover the planet's surface. The Moon moves surprisingly fast, and even the large disc of Jupiter is totally covered within about 80 seconds.

▲ A photograph taken near Last Quarter, showing the terminator passing near the Caucasus (upper) and Apennine mountain ranges. The 83-kilometre crater Archimedes, in the Mare Imbrium, is almost in darkness. Part of the Mare Serenitatis lies to the lower right.

Observing Occultations

First of all you need to know when occultations are expected: the information on page 172 tells you how to obtain occultation predictions.

Occultations of stars brighter than about 6th magnitude can be observed with a 60-millimetre aperture telescope, provided the Moon is not too near the Full and there is no haze. To find the exact time at which a star disappeared,

you will also need a stop-watch and the use of a telephone. Using the stop-watch, press the button at the moment the star disappears; then dial the telephone number of the speaking clock. Stop the watch on a time signal – any one will do. Subtract the time shown on the watch from the time given by the telephone clock to obtain the instant of occultation.

Do pass your observations on to the local society. Much useful information about the motion of the Moon has been collected from occultation observations.

The Moon

Amateur Observation

Thanks to the *Apollo* landings in 1969-1972, we know a great deal more about the Moon's surface and interior than could ever have been found out from the Earth. But the discoveries have been less sensational than those made about the planets, simply because we have such an excellent view of our satellite.

Even the naked eye will reveal the dark lava plains or *maria* ('seas'), and the bright uplands. Brilliant individual patches such as the white deposit around Copernicus (Lunar Chart 3) can also be discerned.

It is interesting to compare the naked-eye view with a chart, and to discover how much small detail can be seen. The bright crater Kepler (Chart 3) is more difficult than Copernicus, but the dark central sea Mare Vaporum (Chart 2) is harder still.

Remember that the charts show an inverted view of the Moon, to agree with the upside-down view of most astronomical telescopes.

▶ **The craters** Fracastorius (lower) and Piccolomini are shown within the white outline in relation to the waxing crescent Moon. The enlargement (opposite, lower right) allows comparison to be made with a drawing of Piccolomini (opposite) by an amateur atronomer using a 200 millimetre telescope. The stages from outline to completion can be seen.

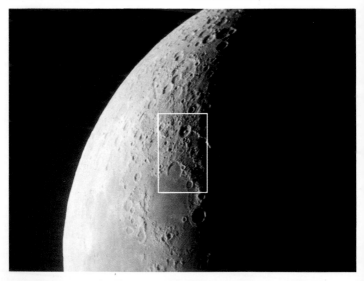

100

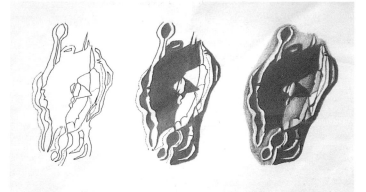

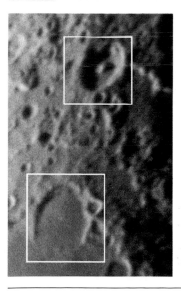

Binoculars or a low-power telescope show the main lunar features perfectly well, but for an adequate view of the craters and mountain chains in their true majesty, an aperture of 75 millimetres or more and a magnification of at least 100 is necessary. This gives a breathtaking view of the lunar surface.

The Lunar Charts

For convenience, the Earth-turned surface shown on the charts that follow has been divided into four quadrants. Objects in the 1st and 2nd quadrants are best observed between New and First Quarter, when the Sun is rising over them, and again between Full and Last Quarter, when the Sun is setting.

The 3rd and 4th quadrants can be seen under sunrise illumination between First Quarter and Full, and under sunset conditions between Last Quarter and New Moon.

The Moon

Lunar Chart 1
South-East Quadrant

To aid identification, the objects on these charts are shown as they would appear under sunset illumination, when they lie near the terminator.

Rheita Valley: Best seen at four days old, this 160-kilometre long fault is never very easy to make out because of its tumbled neighbourhood.

Altai Mountains: One of the more prominent mountain ranges in this quadrant. They look rather like the border of a wide scooped-out valley, and rise in places to 4000 metres.

Theophilus. This crater, 100 kilometres across, has overlapped its neighbour Cyrillus, proving that it was formed at a later date.

Fracastorius: A good example of an old crater whose wall has been partly melted and broken down by fresh lava from the newly formed Mare Nectaris.

Petavius: This makes an imposing sight with Vendelinus, Langrenus and Furnerius along the terminator of the three-day-old Moon. Measuring 160 kilometres across, it has a wide valley running from the central mountain to the south-west wall.

Hipparchus: This and its neighbour **Albategnius** are both about 150 kilometres across and bear all the signs of extreme age, having been peppered by meteoritic impacts long after they were first formed by gigantic collisions early in the solar system's history.

Stöfler: Prominent because of the intrusions on its east wall, this 80-kilometre crater can be recognized quite easily even in the chaotic terrain that characterizes the southern lunar highlands.

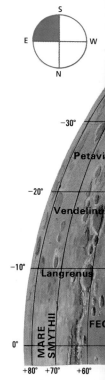

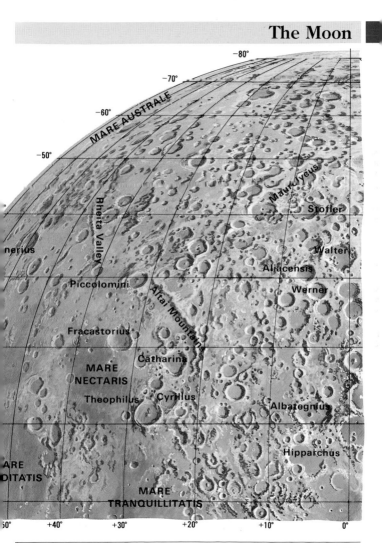

-80°
-70°
-60°
MARE AUSTRALE
-50°
Mauilyeus
Stofler
nerius
Walter
Aliacensis
Piccolomini
Werner
Altai Mountains
Fracastorius
Catharina
MARE
NECTARIS
Cyrillus
Theophilus
Albategnius
Rheita Valley
Hipparchus
ARE
DITATIS
MARE
TRANQUILLITATIS
50°   +40°   +30°   +20°   +10°   0°

Lunar Chart 2
North-East Quadrant

Cleomedes: A magnificent 130-kilometre crater, spectacular about two days after Full, when it and the Mare Crisium make a superb sight.

Mare Crisium: One of the smaller seas, only 500 kilometres across, but very prominent. Its distance from the East limb changes markedly throughout the month, due to the Moon's *libration* – a slight swinging on its axis due to its changing orbital velocity getting out of step with its constant axial spin. Libration allows an observer to see a small part of the 'invisible' hemisphere.

Mare Serenitatis: A partly mountain-bordered sea, best seen at about five days old, when the surface is seen to be crossed by numerous ridges, as if it had wrinkled like a skin over the still-warm interior.

Bessel: A small crater, only about 20 kilometres across, but easily spotted on the relatively crater-free surface of the Mare Serenitatis. A long bright ray crosses both it and the mare.

Endymion: Compare the dark floor of this 130-kilometre crater with its lighter neighbours Atlas and Hercules.

Caucasus Mountains: These and the Apennines are among the highest, rising in places to over 6000 metres. They mark the boundary between the Mare Serenitatis and the Mare Imbrium.

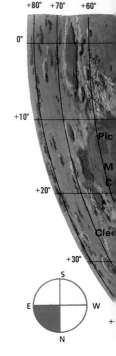

Hyginus Rille: A long valley, visible at First Quarter as a thread-like line if a small telescope is used.

Alpine Valley: The Alps are not the highest mountain range on the Moon, but they contain the most extraordinary valley, 130 kilometres long and over 10 kilometres wide. At First Quarter it is visible with a 60-millimetre telescope as a sharp cut.

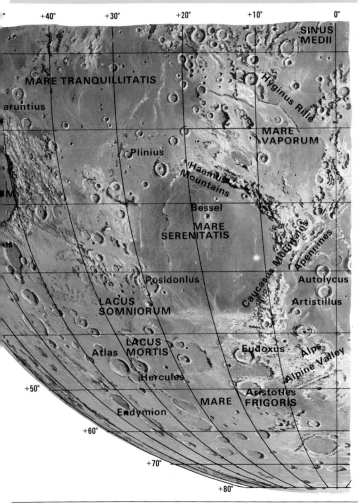

+40°   +30°   +20°   +10°   0°

SINUS MEDII

MARE TRANQUILLITATIS

aruntius

Hyginus Rille

MARE VAPORUM

Plinius

Haemus Mountains

Bessel

MARE SERENITATIS

Caucasus Mountains

Apennines

Posidonius

Autolycus

LACUS SOMNIORUM

Artistillus

LACUS MORTIS

Atlas

Eudoxus

Alps

Alpine Valley

Hercules

Aristoteles

MARE FRIGORIS

+50°

Endymion

+60°

+70°

+80°

105

The Moon

Lunar Chart 3
North-West Quadrant

Plato: A beautiful dark-floored crater 100 kilometres across. Evidently the interior was flooded by re-melting.

Archimedes: This fine 90-kilometre crater, with its smaller companions Autolycus and Aristillus, makes a fine sight just after First Quarter. The floors of all three have been re-melted, presumably by the same action that produced the Mare Imbrium.

Mare Imbrium: Perhaps the most beautiful of all the seas, as well as being one of the largest, measuring about 800 kilometres across.

Straight Range: A small but obvious mountain group that stands up conspicuously on the Mare surface near Plato.

Sinus Iridum: Probably once a huge crater 250 kilometres across, but now one wall has been reduced by flooding, leaving a magnificent bay with peaks (the Jura Mountains) rising to 6000 metres. When the Moon is about nine and a half days old they can be seen with the naked eye, jutting over the terminator.

Copernicus: One of the youngest large craters on the Moon. Ninety kilometres across, it shows all the characteristic features: terraced walls, surrounding ridges and pits from the impact, a central peak, and the white rays caused by glassy molten fragments that soared

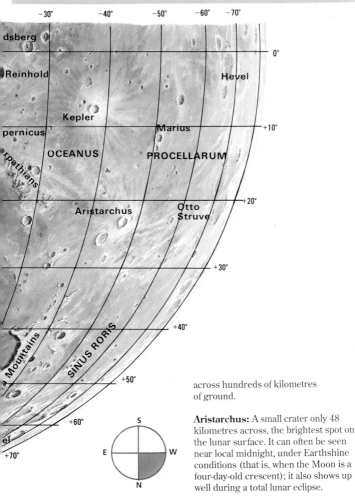

-30°   -40°   -50°   -60°   -70°

dsberg

Reinhold   Hevel   0°

Kepler   +10°

pernicus   Marius

OCEANUS   PROCELLARUM

Aristarchus   Otto
                Struve   +20°

                                                         +30°

                                                         +40°

SINUS RORIS

a Mountains   +50°

                                                         +60°

el
+70°

across hundreds of kilometres
of ground.

Aristarchus: A small crater only 48
kilometres across, the brightest spot on
the lunar surface. It can often be seen
near local midnight, under Earthshine
conditions (that is, when the Moon is a
four-day-old crescent); it also shows up
well during a total lunar eclipse.

The Moon

Lunar Chart 4
South-West Quadrant

Clavius: One of the largest lunar craters, 230 kilometres across, with a chain of more recently-formed craters inside it.

Ptolemaeus: This ruined 145-kilometre crater, together with Alphonsus and Arzachel, are imposing just after the First Quarter; the western walls are sunlit long before their bases are fully illuminated.

Oceanus Procellarum: The largest sea, but without mountainous borders, and much of it is rather featureless with a small aperture. There are many drowned rings where ancient craters have been submerged.

Grimaldi: A very dark crater near the west limb, and always obvious because of it stint. The slightly smaller neighbour Riccioli (160 kilometres across) is much harder to make out, except just before Full, when it lies on the terminator.

Gassendi: A beautiful crater with a flooded floor 90 kilometres across. Amateurs study Gassendi closely, because faint temporary red colorations have been reported in this area.

Mare Humorum: One of the better-defined small seas. A fine sight on the 11-day-old Moon, when tiny craterlets and ridges seam the surface.

Schickard: A dark-floored 210-kilometre crater, ruined by later impacts.

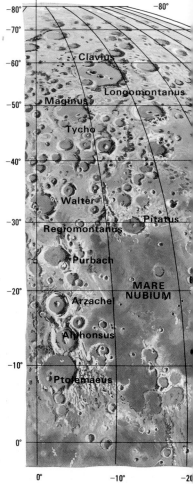

108

The Moon

Note the curious object Wargentin to the south-west: a unique plateau, apparently caused when the original crater became filled with lava.

Tycho: A well-formed crater 90 kilometres across, obviously a relatively recent, well-preserved formation like Copernicus, and the centre of the most extensive ray system on the Moon.

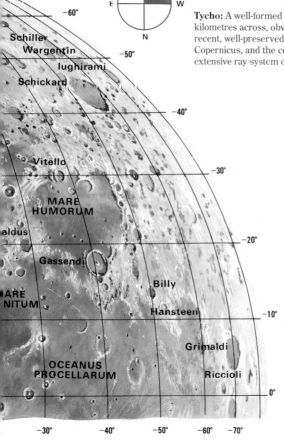

-70°

-60°

S

E

W

N

-50°

Schiller

Wargentin

Iughirami

-40°

Schickard

Vitello

-30°

MARE
HUMORUM

-20°

aldus

Gassendi

ARE
NITUM

Billy

Hansteen

-10°

Grimaldi

OCEANUS
PROCELLARUM

Riccioli

0°

-30°   -40°   -50°   -60°   -70°

The Planets

The planets have been mysterious objects ever since the ancient astronomers puzzled about their movements across the celestial sphere. We now understand their wanderings; but as 'worlds' there are still many questions unanswered about them.

The planets can be divided into two groups: the small or *terrestrial* planets, Mercury, Venus, Earth, Mars and possibly Pluto, whose mass is in their solid globes; and the four *giant* planets, Jupiter, Saturn, Uranus and Neptune, which consist predominantly of gas and have little or no rocky material.

The planets, satellites, comets and scraps of debris that make up the Sun's family were all formed, together with our star, inside a huge cloud that probably consisted of 90 per cent hydrogen, 9 per cent helium, and just traces of the other 90 naturally-occurring elements.

Hydrogen and helium have very fast-moving atoms that require a strong gravitational pull to restrain them. The Sun, and the giant planets – Jupiter, Saturn, Uranus and Neptune – were able to do so, and consist mostly of hydrogen. The smaller planets, like the Earth, lost their hydrogen very early on and are dense, rocky bodies.

Planet Fragments

Many other bodies also condensed from the original solar nebula. Some became satellites of the planets, while other smaller relics are the thousands of minor planets or *asteroids*, orbiting mainly in the region between Mars and Jupiter. Innumerable millions of dust-sized fragments, *meteoroids,* circle the Sun invisibly unless they burn up as *meteors* in the Earth's atmosphere. Finally there are the curious *comets*, icy and vaporous that brightens to visibility only as they sweep near the Sun during their lonely passage.

A question which intrigues every astronomer is whether there is life on the other planets in the Solar System. Certainly the conditions on most other planets make this unlikely. Their temperatures, for example, are too extreme, fluctuating from severe cold to searing heat, for the plant and animal life of Earth.

This view of the Sun and planets shows how small the Earth is compared with the four 'giant planets'. But even the giants are tiny compared to the Sun.

The nine planets in the Solar System are:

1 Mercury	2 Venus	3 Earth
4 Mars	5 Jupiter	6 Saturn
7 Uranus	8 Neptune	9 Pluto

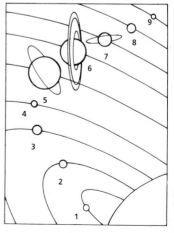

SOLAR SYSTEM FACTS

Planet	Distance from Sun (m. of km) Min	Mean	Max	Diameter (km)	Length of day		Length of year	No. of satellites
Mercury	46	58	70	4850		176d	88d	0
Venus	107½	108	109	12,104		114d	225d	0
Earth	147	149½	152	12,756		24h	365d	1
Mars	206½	228	249	6790	24h	37m	687d	2
Jupiter	741	778½	815½	142,600	9h	50m	11.9y	16
Saturn	1347	1427	1507	120,200	10h	14m	29.5y	18
Uranus	2735	2870	3004	51,000	17h	18m	84y	15
Neptune	4456	4497	4537	49,500	16h	7m	165y	8
Pluto	4425	5900	7357	2280	6d	9h	248y	1

▲ **Spacecraft** have photographed many planets and satellites. The results suggest that every solid surface in the Solar System, including the Earth's, was bombarded by small interplanetary bodies in its early history. The photograph above is of Mercury's surface.

▶ **The surface** of Mars as seen from a *Viking* spacecraft.

◀ **A satellite** view of Mount Etna, Sicily. The radiation from different kinds of rock, soil and vegetation, as well as human settlements, can be converrted into false colours to aid mapping of surface resources.

113

The Planets

Observing the Planets

The planets are always fascinating to watch. Due to their orbital motion around the Sun, they are never in exactly the same position on the celestial sphere from night to night. However, different planets move in different ways.

Inferior and Superior Planets

Mercury and Venus, which are called the *inferior planets,* are a special case. Their orbits lie inside that of the Earth, and so they are always in the neighbourhood of the Sun. Pretending, for simplicity, that the Earth is stationary, the lower left diagram shows how these planets move. First they pass from invisibility on the far side of the Sun, a position called *superior conjunction*, to eastern elongation, visible in the western sky after sunset. Then they go through inferior conjunction again, usually invisible, and

out to western or morning elongation. During this time they pass through phases like the Moon, appearing Full near superior conjunction and as a thin crescent near inferior conjunction.

The other planets behave as in the right-hand diagram. When closest to the Earth they are opposite the Sun in the sky, like the Full Moon – a position known as opposition; near conjunction they are invisible, behind the Sun. Only Mars sometimes shows a slight phase, near quadrature. These planets, from Mars to Pluto, are known as the *superior planets*.

The planets from Mercury to Saturn are visible with the naked eye; Uranus and Neptune can be seen with binoculars. Only Pluto is invisible without a proper astronomical telescope of about 250 millimetres aperture. Binoculars will reveal the crescent phase

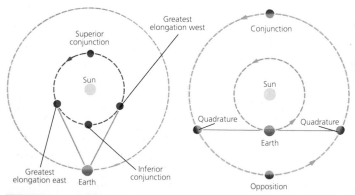

INFERIOR PLANET

Superior conjunction

Sun

Greatest elongation west

Greatest elongation east

Inferior conjunction

Earth

SUPERIOR PLANET

Conjunction

Sun

Quadrature

Quadrature

Earth

Opposition

of Venus and up to four moons of Jupiter, as well as one of Saturn's moons. Binoculars are also a great help in finding shy Mercury during its fleeting appearances.

Apparent path

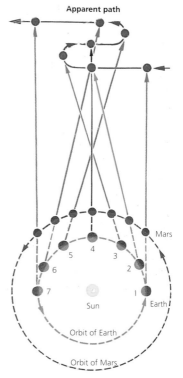

▼ **Binoculars** or a small telescope should reveal Jupiter's four large moons when they are near elongation from the planet.

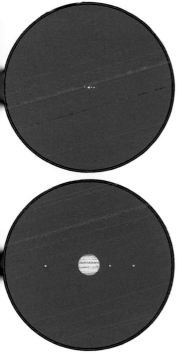

▲ **A powerful astronomical** telescope will enable you to see a mass of fine, constantly-changing detail on Jupiter's disc.

▲ **When Mars**, or any other superior planet, comes to opposition, the Earth's greater orbital speed makes it appear to backtrack or retrograde for a few weeks, just as a car being passed seems to be travelling backwards. This retrograde motion was one of the chief problems faced by the Earth-centred system of Ptolemy (page 22). The positions at 3 and 5, when the planet slows down and reverses direction, are known as 'stationary points'.

The Planets

Mercury

Mercury lies within 28 degrees of the Sun, and from temperate latitudes it can be seen only in twilight, when it is near elongation. From the northern hemisphere, the best time for hunting it is from January to April as an evening object, and from July to October as a morning object. In the southern hemisphere, these times are reversed.

Finding Mercury

Look about ten degrees above the Sun's place about three-quarters of an hour before sunrise or after sunset. Times of forthcoming elongations are given in the Sky Diary (pp. 160-162). But start looking for the planet about ten days before the time given. Mercury is white but if you are looking for it in the evening, the sky often colours it pink.

Mercury shows such a tiny disc that a magnification of 250 shows it only as large as the naked-eye Moon. It was not until *Mariner* 10 visited it in 1974-1975 that much was found out about it.

We now know that it is crater-ridden like the Moon. Its surface, alternately baking and freezing, is airless and dead.

▼ **Mercury** sometimes transits the Sun at inferior conjunction. This photograph was taken on November 10, 1973. The next transit will be on November 15, 1999.

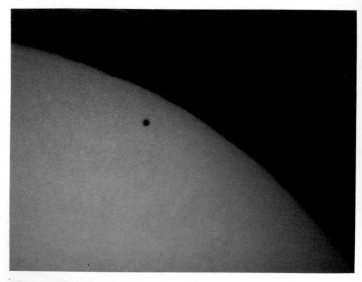

Core

Mantle

Crust

MERCURY FACTS

Surface temperature: 350°C/–170°C
Gravity: 0 38 X Earth
Density: 5 4 X water
Atmosphere: none
Apparent diameter:
9″ (inferior conjunction);
6″ (superior conjunction)
Interval between inferior conjunctions:
116 days
Maximum magnitude: –1 4

▲ **Mercury** has an exceptionally large metal core, which makes it the densest planet in the solar system after the Earth.

The Planets

Venus

Like Mercury, Venus is an inferior planet, swinging into and out of the Sun's rays. It is much easier to see, however, and near elongation it can be made out with the naked eye in the daylight sky.

Phase and Markings

Between elongation and inferior conjunction, the crescent phase can be seen using firmly-mounted binoculars. It is brightest in the mid-crescent stage, and this is the best time to seek it with the naked eye in daylight, perhaps at a morning elongation as the Sun rises.

It is no use observing Venus through a telescope in a dark sky, because its brilliance dazzles. The best time is in bright dawn or dusk, when it begins to be easily detectable with the naked eye. Cloud markings are very difficult to see, but occasionally observers have recorded hazy details that seem to conform to the streaks recorded by spacecraft. A blue photographic filter placed near the eyepiece should improve the contrast of any visible clouds.

Due to the way the atmosphere shades off near the terminator, the phase of Venus is usually slightly less than predicted – on the date of the half-phase, for example, it may appear slightly concave rather than perfectly straight.

Rapid Movement

Venus is usually lost from view for about four months around the time of superior conjunction. But it sweeps through inferior conjunction so quickly that it reappears in the morning sky only a matter of days after vanishing in the evening twilight. Venus is called the Morning or Evening Star according to when it is visible.

▼ **The Phases of Venus.** Near inferior junction, when it appears as a thin crescent, Venus is about six times closer than at inferior conjunction. Therefore, although only a part of the illuminated surface is turned towards the Earth, the crescent phase appeals most to amateur observers.

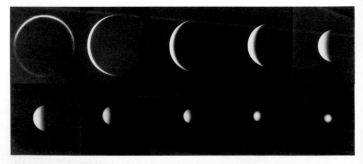

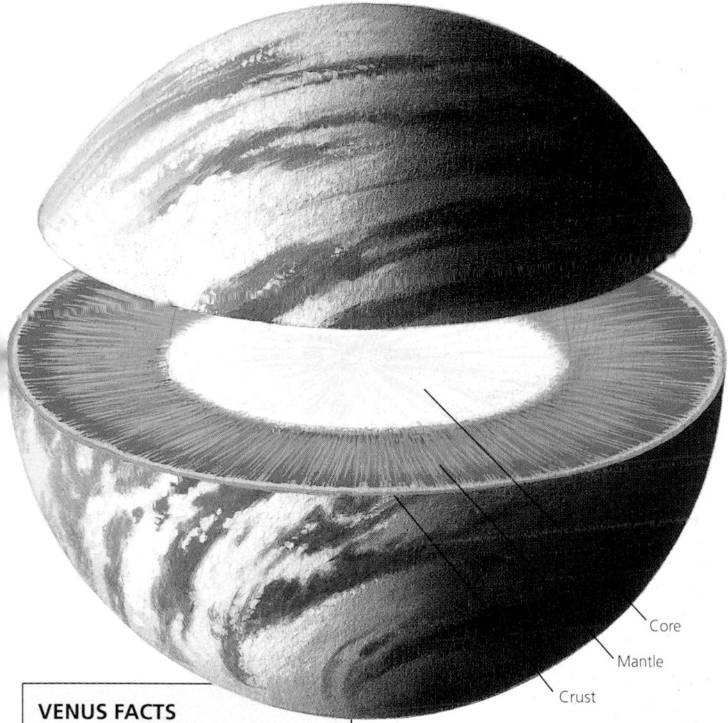

Core

Mantle

Crust

VENUS FACTS

Surface temperature: 480°C
Gravity: 0.9 X Earth
Density: 5.2 X water
Atmosphere: mainly carbon dioxide
Atmospheric pressure: 91 X Earth's
Apparent diameter:
    62″ (inferior conjunction):
    10″ (superior conjunction)
Interval between inferior conjunctions:
    584 days
Maximum magnitude: −4.4

▲ **Venus'** internal structure is probably similar to that of the Earth, but its surface has proved a puzzle. There is evidence that its crust may have completely melted a few hundred million years ago, erasing all the older features.

119

Mars

Mars is the only planet in the Solar System that gives us a reasonable view of its true surface. But because it is so rarely well-placed for observation, it has puzzled rather than informed amateur and professional astronomers alike.

Mars comes to opposition every 26 months or so, but its orbit is so eccentric that some apparitions bring the planet much close than do others. In 1971 it came within 56 million kilometres of Earth, but in 1980 its opposition distance was about 100 million kilometres.

Observation Hints
This means that observing Mars is a frustrating business. Really favourable oppositions occur at intervals of about 17 years: the last was in 1986. Mars also approaches and recedes so rapidly that

▼ **The face of Mars**. Images from the 1976 *Viking Orbiter* spacecraft, showing the system of canyons known as the Valles Marineris.

▼ **Mars** has a relatively small metallic core.

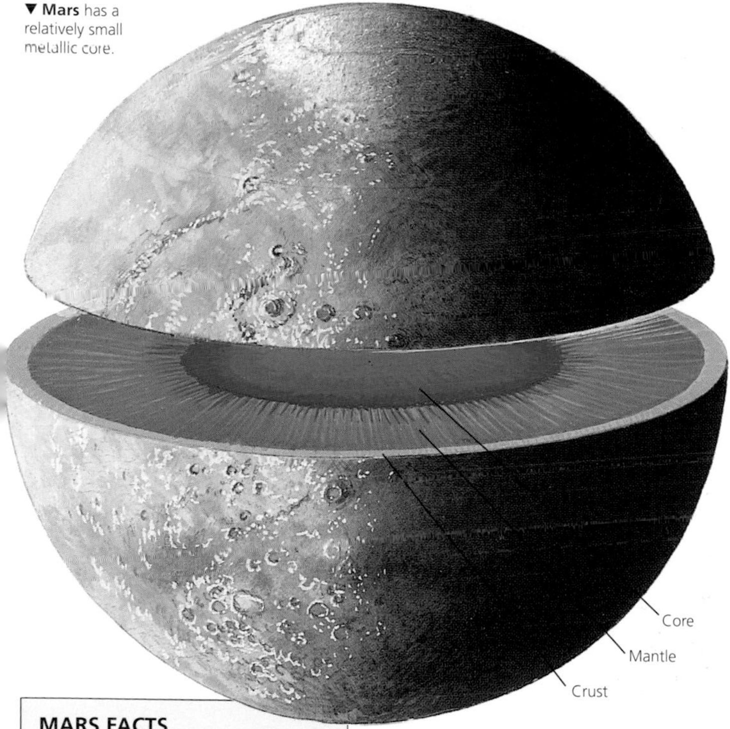

Core
Mantle
Crust

MARS FACTS

Surface temperature: −20°C/−200°C
Gravity: 0.38 X Earth
Density: 3.95 X water]
Atmosphere: very thin, mainly carbon dioxide
Apparent diameter:
14″–25″ (opposition);
3″ (conjunction)
Interval between oppositions: 780 days
Maximum magnitude: −2.5

useful work can be carried only for a few weeks. When it does appear, you can try to follow its rapid path with binoculars. With telescopes of 60 millimetre aperture you can look out for dark markings and the polar caps. Try following a dark marking for about an hour. It will move with the planet's rotation from east to west (right to left in the telescope).

The Planets

The Deceptive Planet

In 1886, the American observer, Percival Lowell, built an observatory in Arizona dedicated to the study of Mars. This was a time when astronomers had little idea of the conditions on other planets, and Mars was widely thought of as an earthlike world, where intelligent life could thrive. Lowell believed that he had discovered dozens of artificial waterways or canals on its surface, and that the planet was inhabited by intelligent beings. Unfortunately, the thin straight lines observed by Lowell and others do not exist. The tiny Martian disc had deceived them into imagining these features.

Mars' Atmosphere

The atmosphere of Mars is very thin – less than a hundredth the density of our own – and consists mainly of carbon dioxide. But fierce winds can blow the dust into huge clouds, visible from the Earth by the dark features they obliterate; even the polar caps have sometimes disappeared. The strongest dust storms happen when Mars is near perihelion, at its closest to the Sun.

White clouds are also seen, usually near the planet's limb, where they can be almost as bright as a polar cap. Like the caps, they consist of ice. There could also be a good deal of water below the surface, permanently frozen.

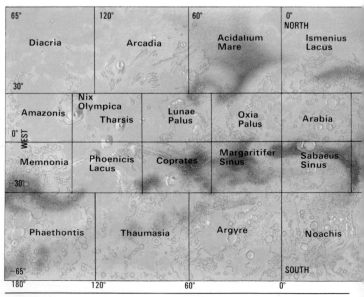

The Planets

Life on Mars

Today, even after the sensational *Viking* landings in 1976, we still have not finally answered the question whether there is life on Mars. If there is, though, it can only be on the bacterial level. However, Mars may have been warmer and damper in the past

The two sites that were examined gave no definite evidence of living organisms. But the surface of Mars is so varied – parts are cratered desert, like the Moon, while others exhibit relatively recent volcanic features – that some other regions may be more hospitable. The Mars *Pathfinder* probe is due to land in July 1997.

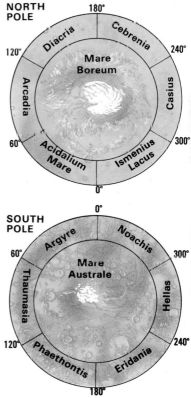

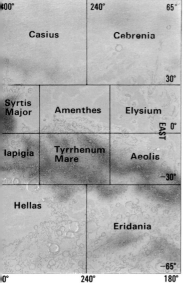

These maps show the surface of Mars as photographed by space probes. The dark areas visible from Earth are shaded in. Two of the most obvious features are the dark Syrtis Major and the light Hellas. The huge volcano on the Tharsis-Amazonis ridge, Nix Olympica, is some 30 kilometres high with a crater at the top 65 kilometres across.

123

The Planets

Jupiter

Jupiter is an ideal planet for the amateur to observe. Its disc is always large (even a magnification of about forty makes it look as big as the Moon), and there are four bright satellites. In order outward from the planet these are Io, Europa, Ganymede and Callisto. They can all be seen using good binoculars.

With an aperture of 60 millimetres and a magnification of one hundred or so, details are visible on the 'surface' (really the upper cloud layer). The belts show wisps and irregularities, and the famous Great Red Spot can be seen when it is prominent, although it sometimes fades from view.

Jupiter spins so rapidly that its disc is noticeably flattened at the poles. A watch of between five and ten minutes will show that its markings are moving from east to west across the disc, due to its rotation. The longitude of a cloud feature can be worked out by timing the moment when it crosses the planet's central line or meridian.

Observing the Satellites

You can also observe the four largest satellites as they move around the planet. Try timing their orbital paths by seeing how long they take to return to a position chosen. Try to make out their shadows as they move across Jupiter's disc.

▼ **Jupiter** may have a rocky or metallic core about the size of the Earth, but it is principally made of hydrogen, compressed into a liquid by the enormous pressure of the outer layers.

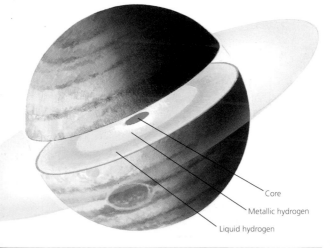

Core

Metallic hydrogen

Liquid hydrogen

JUPITER FACTS

Temperature at cloud tops: −150°C
Gravity: 2 7 X Earth
Density: 1 3 X water
Overall composition: hydrogen, helium
Apparent diameter:
47″ (opposition);
32″ (conjunction)
Intervals between oppositions:
399 days
Maximum magnitude: −2 5

▲ **Jupiter** viewed from a *Voyager* spacecraft, showing the Great Red Spot and one of the satellites. The immense amount of detail here cannot be duplicated by any Earthbound telescope, but these 'brilliant glimpses' do not challenge the long-term monitoring of its cloud changes by a small team of dedicated amateurs.

The Planets

Saturn

Saturn used to be known as the planet with the rings, but we now know that it shares this distinction with Jupiter, Uranus and Neptune. However, the rings around these other planets are so faint that they have never been seen by eye, whereas Saturn's are one of the glories of the night sky.

Earth-based telescopes can distinguish three main rings, but the two *Voyager* spacecraft have revealed hundreds of strands only a few kilometres wide; some are concentric while others are braided together.

The rings lie in the plane of Saturn's equator. Its axis is tilted, so that during its long 'year' we see the rings at different angles. In 1995 they appeared edge-on, while in 2003 their southern surface will be tilted at its widest angle towards the Earth.

Markings and Moons

Saturn's globe is even more flattened than Jupiter's. Its rotation period is slightly longer, but it has very little

rigidity – its average density is less than that of water. The belts are much fainter than those of Jupiter, and noticeable spots are rare. Saturn's most characteristic feature is the occasional production of a large white cloud in its northern hemisphere. A famous one was seen in 1933, while other very prominent ones were observed in 1960 and 1990 – the latter was discovered by amateur observers in time for it to be photographed by the Space Telescope. The intervals between these outbreaks is approximately equal to Saturn's year, and they occur when the northern hemisphere is near 'midsummer'. At least 18 satellites have been discovered – 9 by spacecraft – ranging from Titan, 5200 kilometres across, to objects smaller than many asteroids.

▶ **Two close-up** views from *Voyager* of Saturn and its rings, showing the numerous ringlets.

▼ **Spacecraft** have discovered additional ring zones around Saturn: only the bright A, B and C rings are readibly visible from the Earth.

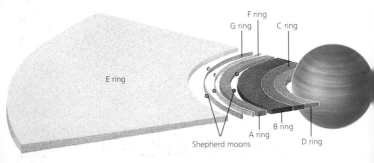

F ring

G ring

C ring

E ring

Shepherd moons

A ring

B ring

D ring

The Planets

Observing Saturn

With the naked eye, Saturn looks like a yellowish star of about magnitude 2. As it takes almost 30 years to pass around the Zodiac once, it spends over two years in each constellation. The 1996 opposition occurs in Pices, and by the year 2000 it will only have moved as far as the neighbouring constellation Aries.

Saturn's rings can be made out with a magnification of around 50, unless they are almost edge-on, as happened in 1995. At this time they can briefly disappear from view in the largest telescopes, making the planet look like a small, flattened Jupiter. When they are wide open, Cassini's Division can be made out in a small astronomical telescope. Titan can be made out with good binoculars, and other moons can be identified with anything more powerful. Apart from a brighter equatorial zone and the dusky poles, it is usually difficult to make out any markings on the disc itself.

SATURN FACTS

Ring system – Outer diameter: 272,300
Inner diameter: 149,300
Temperature at cloud tops: −180°C
Gravity: 1·2 X Earth
Density: 0·7 X water
Overall composition: hydrogen, helium
Apparent diameter of globe:
19½″ (opposition);
16″ (conjunction)
Interval between oppositions: 378 days
Maximum magnitude: −0·3

▼ **Saturn is** probably built on a very similar pattern to Jupiter.

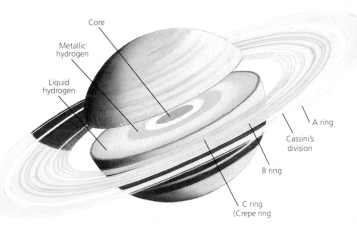

Core

Metallic hydrogen

Liquid hydrogen

A ring

Cassini's division

B ring

C ring (Crepe ring

Uranus, Neptune and Pluto

Our knowledge of Uranus and Neptune used to be scanty. However, from *Voyager 2* we have gained information about these two planets, such as their rotation periods and diameters. We still do not know much about Pluto.

Uranus is just visible to the naked eye, but it was not noticed until 1781.

The discovery was made by William Herschel, who came across the planet in a survey of the sky with a 150-millimetre reflector. The belief that there were just five planets went back thousands of years, so at first Herschel found it hard to believe what he had found.

Neptune and Pluto were found after deliberate searches by astronomers who thought that the gravitational attraction of one or more unseen bodies was pulling Uranus from its theoretical position. Predictions by Adams and Leverrier led to the discovery of Neptune in 1846, and Pluto was found by Tombaugh in 1930.

▼ **A drawing** of the distant planets (not to scale). From right to left: Neptune, Pluto and uranus.

Uranus

Pluto

Neptune

The Planets

Rings and Satellites

Both Uranus and Neptune seem to be built on the giant-planet pattern. They each have small solid cores with thick layers of hydrogen, helium and methane (a compound of hydrogen and carbon) forming an icy, slushy covering. Both planets have narrow ring systems. The axis of Uranus is tilted over so far that each of its poles in turn almost faces the Sun for a while during its long year.

Uranus has 15 known moons and Neptune has eight. One of Neptune's moons, Triton, is slightly larger than our Moon, and *Voyager* 2 recorded jets of nitrogen gas spurting up from its surface. Winds tear through the outer methane atmosphere of Neptune at up to 2200 kilometres per hour.

Little Pluto has a curious satellite called Charon, half its own diameter. The orbit of Pluto is so eccentric that between 1979 and 1999 it is closer than Neptune to the Sun. In 1992 the first of several small, as yet unnamed bodies was discovered beyond Pluto.

Observation Hints

Both Uranus and Neptune can be made out with binoculars if their position in the sky is known. But you will need to refer to astronomical yearbooks (see page 172) to know in which part of the sky to start hunting for them.

▲ **The face** of Uranus shows an unbroken haze in this photograph taken by *Voyager* 2 in January 1986.

◀ **Neptune** is revealed in detail by *Voyager* 2 in August 1989. Bright, wispy clouds are shown overlying the Great Dark Spot at its southern margin and over its northwest boundary.

▶ **Pluto** is smaller than our Moon and denser than any of its neighbours. It is often referred to as a double planet because of is very large moon, Charon. Pluto is the only planet not to have been visited by a fly-by spacecraft.

Solar System Debris

The planets of the Solar System formed when tiny particles inside the solar nebula began adhering together. In some cases the process was halted before it had gone very far, and small bodies a few kilometres across were all that resulted. Larger bodies probably collided, and broke up. The result of these misfortunes is the zone of asteroids or minor planets, which lies between the orbits of Mars and Jupiter.

Asteroids

The largest asteroid, Ceres, is 1000 kilometres across, but most of the 5000 that have been discovered are far smaller. Vesta, 540 kilometres across, can sometimes reach 6th magnitude, and about a dozen can be seen with binoculars. A few asteroids orbit near the Earth: in December 1994 an object the size of a house, 1994XM, missed our planet by only 100,000 kilometres.

▲ **This brilliant fireball** was accidentally caught by an amateur photographing the stars.

Observing Asteroids

An asteroid can be distinguished from a star only by its nightly motion, or by using a good star atlas. If its approximate position in the sky is known, an accurate drawing of the field will show one 'star' to have shifted. Asteroids will also show up as short streaks in long-exposure photographs taken anywhere near the ecliptic.

▼ **Gaspra,** an object about 20 kilometres long, became the first asteroid to be photographed in detail when the *Galileo* spacecraft passed it in October 1991 on its way to Jupiter.

Our moon (*to scale*)   Ceres

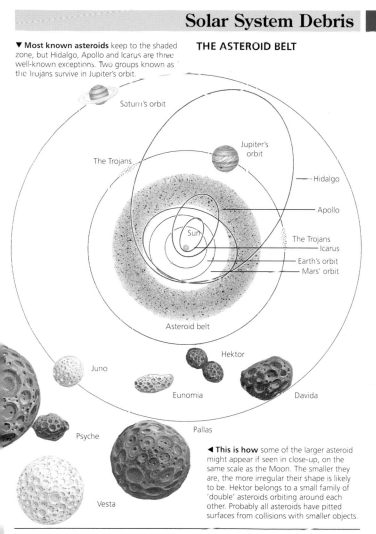

▼ **Most known asteroids** keep to the shaded zone, but Hidalgo, Apollo and Icarus are three well-known exceptions. Two groups known as the Trojans survive in Jupiter's orbit.

THE ASTEROID BELT

Saturn's orbit

Jupiter's orbit

The Trojans

Hidalgo

Apollo

Sun

The Trojans
Icarus
Earth's orbit
Mars' orbit

Asteroid belt

Hektor

Juno

Eunomia

Davida

Psyche

Pallas

◄ **This is how** some of the larger asteroid might appear if seen in close-up, on the same scale as the Moon. The smaller they are, the more irregular their shape is likely to be. Hektor belongs to a small family of 'double' asteroids orbiting around each other. Probably all asteroids have pitted surfaces from collisions with smaller objects.

Vesta

Meteors

Meteroids – fragments of solid matter not more than a few centimetres across – pervade the Solar System. Some orbit the Sun independently, while others travel in swarms that have scattered themselves along a particular orbit.

The Earth moves in its orbit at about 30 kilometres per second, and when it encounters a meteroid, the relative velocity of the two bodies can be up to about 60 kilometres per second if it is a head-on collision. At these higher speeds the meteroid is vaporized in the atmosphere, leaving the streak we see as a shooting star or *meteor.*

Individual objects produce *sporadic* meteors. When the Earth passes through a swarm, however, a so-called meteor *shower* occurs. This recurs every year when the Earth returns to its intersection with the swarm. An estimated million tonnes of interplanetary dust and meteroid debris reaches the Earth every day.

The Earth sometimes collides with much larger bodies weighing several kilogrammes. These leave a brilliant streak that lights up the whole landscape, and may even reach the ground as a *meteorite.*

◀ **This photograph** shows the tracks of numerous meteors that flashed across the sky during the brilliant Leonid display of November 1966. Such brilliant displays are very rare.

▼ **Meteor swarms** may be the dust of disrupted comets. A meteor shower is seen when the Earth passes through this material scattered along the orbit.

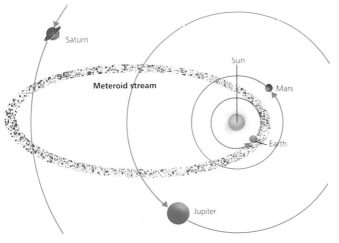

Saturn

Meteroid stream

Sun

Mars

Earth

Jupiter

Solar System Debris

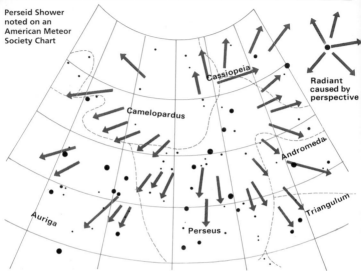

Perseid Shower noted on an American Meteor Society Chart

Cassiopeia

Camelopardus

Radiant caused by perspective

Andromeda

Auriga

Perseus

Triangulum

Observing Meteors

Sporadic meteors can be seen on any clear night, being most frequent and brighter in the early morning. Meteor showers, however, occur only at certain times of the year – see the table opposite. Bright moonlight can drown the fainter meteors, so observations are affected by the Moon's phases.

Observing a meteor shower is even more fun, since a group of up to six observers is best. Four people are allotted a quarter of the lower sky each, one looks directly overhead, and the sixth writes down details of the meteors they've seen.

The most useful data to record are the time (to within half a minute), magnitude, speed (fast, medium or slow), colour, and whether a train (a faint after-trail) was left. It is also interesting to work out how many meteors per hour were seen (the Hourly Rate or HR).

Experienced observers can try noting the meteor paths in relation to the stars. Shower meteors all appear to come from one place in the sky – the *radiant*. The constellation in which the radiant lies gives the meteor shower its name. Often observers prepare in advance charts, like the one above, on which meteor paths can be marked.

▶ **The Meteor Crater** in Arizona may be 50,000 years old. It is 1300 metres in diameter. On the Moon, because of its lower gravity, the same impact would have produced a much larger crater.

METEOR SHOWERS

Some meteor showers have very sharp maxima that lasts only a few hours, and these times vary from year to year because of leap-year adjustments. The Sky Diary (pp. 160-162) gives the best times at which to observe the Quadrantids, April Lyrids, Perseids and Geminids, all of which have brief maxima. The two Aquarid showers are best observed from the southern hemisphere.

Shower	Noticeable activity			Maximum activity		Maximum HR (approx.)
Quadrantids	Jan	1 –	6	Jan	3-4	50
April Lyrids	Apr	19 –	24	Apr	22	10
η Aquarids	May	1 –	8	May	5	10
δ Aquarids	Jul	15 –	Aug 15	Jul	27	25
Perseids	Jul	25 –	Aug 18	Aug	12	50
Orionids	Oct	16 –	26	Oct	20	20
Taurids	Oct	20 –	Nov 30	Nov	8	8
Leonids	Nov	15 –	19	Nov	17	6?
Geminids	Dec	7 –	15	Dec	14	50

Solar System Debris

Comets

The popular idea of a comet is of a long-tailed object gleaming in the sky. But fewer than one in a hundred achieves this distinction. Most are so faint that they can be seen only as a faint smudge, even with a powerful telescope, while countless more must pass through space undetected.

Comets are believed to originate in the Oort Cloud, a 'halo' of millions of bodies at an estimated distance of about 50,000 AU from the Sun. Rarely more than a few kilometres across, these were some of the first condensations within the nebula around the young Sun, and consist principally of light crumbly rock and water ice.

Occasionally, one of these bodies starts to 'fall' towards the Sun, a process taking millions of years. As it heats up the frozen material vapourizes, releasing the crumbly dust it has been cementing together. The dust and vapour form a huge cloud or coma around the solid nucleus, and the Sun's continuous outflow of atomic particles may sweep this material into one or more tails millions of kilometres long. After hurtling round the Sun for a number of years, perhaps even closer than the planet Mercury, the comet recedes back into interstellar space.

▶ **Jupiter's powerful** gravitational influence on comets was demonstrated spectacularly in July 1994. Two years earlier its pull had forced Comet Shoemaker-Levy 9 into a collision course, breaking its nucleus into more than twenty fragments, The photograph shows the 'fireball' in Jupiter's atmosphere soon after one of the fragments impacted.

▶ **One of the most spectacular** comets of the century, Comet West was discovered by Richard West in 1976. For several days in March 1976 it was brighter than any planet except Venus and could be seen with the naked eye. It was clear from its large dust trail that the comet's head was already breaking up.

The comet may return to the Oort Cloud, but it is also possible that the powerful gravity of the Solar System giant planets, particularly Jupiter and Saturn, may deflect it into a much smaller orbit. This is the origin of the 'short-period' comets such as Halley's. Since they have made numerous passages varound the Sun, much of their volatile material has already been blasted away, and they are relatively faint. The really brilliant comets, such as Comet West (1976) or Comet Ikeya-Keki (1965), have never previously been seen in recorded history, and may have been making their first orbit of the Sun since the Solar System began.

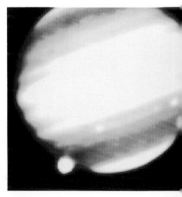

Solar System Debris

Observing Comets

Amateurs are still very successful in hunting for new comets. This involves sweeping regularly over the night sky with an aperture of between about 100 and 200 millimetres, with a low magnification, for example x 30.

Since comets are brightest when near the Sun, the western sky after dusk and the eastern sky before dawn are the most promising areas to search. A very dark transparent sky gives the best chance of making a discovery; but it may take some time. The most successful living comet discoverer is William Bradfield, an Australian amateur, who has so far found sixteen comets.

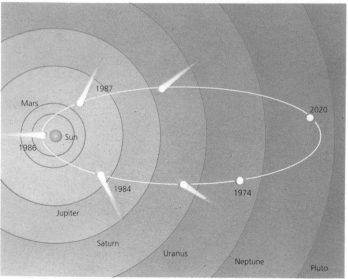

▲ **Halley's Comet** photographed in March 1986, three weeks after passing round the Sun. It appears an average of every 77 years.

◄ **Halley's Comet** passed perihelion in 1986, and will have receded beyond the orbit of Neptune by the year 2020.

▲ **The dark,** irregular nucleus of Halley's Comet, recorded by the *Giotto* space probe in 1986, is about 12 kilometres in length.

SOME IMPORTANT COMETS			
Name	Orbit period (years)	Last seen	Remarks
Encke	3.3	1987	Sometimes visible with binoculars; the shortest period known.
Biela	6.6	1852	Seen to break up. A meteor shower occurred when the Earth next passed its position.
Schwassmann-Wachmann	16.1	–	Always more distant than Jupiter and comes to opposition every year. Occasional outbursts.
Halley	76.0	1986	Last perihelion passage in 1986.
Daylight comet	750?	1882	Probably the brightest comet of modern times.
Donati	1900?	1858	Famous for its curved tail, 40° long.
Daylight comet	4 million?	1910	Probably the brightest comet of the 20th century.

Atmospheric Astronomy

If the Earth had no atmosphere (ignoring the fact that life would then be impossible), the astronomer's task would be much simpler. The sky would always be transparent, and free from clouds, and stars near the horizon would shine as brightly as those overhead.

But some features of the night sky would be absent. *Aurorae* occur in the upper atmosphere, as do the rare *noctilucent* clouds. Other features, which we include under 'atmospheric astronomy' although they really occur out in space, would be seen more clearly, particularly the *Zodiacal Light, Zodiacal Band,* and *Gegenschein* or *Counterglow.*

Aurorae

Aurorae are connected with solar activity. Near ground level, the atmosphere consists of nitrogen, oxygen and other elements existing as stable molecules. But at a height of about 90 kilometres, the air is so thin that the molecules are split into atoms, which are broken down, by the Sun's energy.

When the Sun's surface is particularly active, it radiates atomic particles that become trapped in the Earth's magnetic field, rebounding from pole to pole and striking flashes of light from these high-altitude atoms. The result is an auroral display. Aurorae

▼ **The Earth** has the most powerful magnetic field of all the terrestrial planets. Electrically-charged atomic particles from the Sun are trapped in different shells, or are deflected into a 'bow wave'.

▶ **A bright aurora** is a memorable sight. Displays are most common around the time of sunspot maximum, when the Sun sometimes emits fierce bursts of radiation that makes atoms in the upper atmosphere glow.

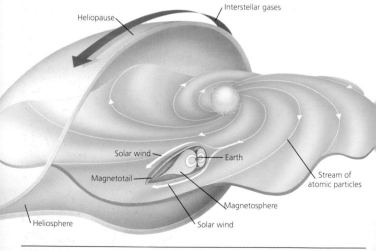

Interstellar gases

Heliopause

Solar wind

Earth

Magnetotail

Stream of atomic particles

Magnetosphere

Heliosphere

Solar wind

occur mostly in the upper atmosphere near the Earth's poles, where the solar particles find an easier entry down through the magnetic field. Aurorae can last for hours and be bright enough to be noticed by non-astronomers.

Observation Notes

A faint aurora usually takes the form of a diffuse glow above the northern horizon (the southern horizon, in the southern hemisphere). It may develop rays extending up towards the zenith, and green and red tints may appear.

If you suspect an auroral display, make regular (for example five-minute) records of its height and extent along the horizon. The best latitude for auroral observations is about 60 degrees north or south, but strong displays can sometimes be seen close to the equator.

Zodiacal Light

Zodiacal Light is caused when sunlight is reflected by inter-planetary dust. It takes the form of a cone extending along the ecliptic. Since it is so faint, it can be seen only during a critical time between the beginning or end of twilight and its own rising or setting.

In higher latitudes it makes a low angle with the horizon, and is difficult to see. In latitudes of about 35 degrees and less, it is bright enough to drown the fainter stars, and is known as the 'false dawn'.

Look for it in the west after dusk in the spring, and in the east just before dawn in the autumn (southern observers should reverse these times). A dark country sky is essential, and your eyes must be thoroughly dark-adapted if the elusive cone is to be seen.

Gegenschein

The Gegenschein is also caused by interplanetary dust, but is lies opposite the Sun in the sky, and appears as a very dim patch several degrees across. It is fainter than the Zodiacal Light or the Milky Way. The best time to observe it is around midnight. In the northern hemisphere look for it at the beginning of November, when it lies in Aries (Star Maps 2 and 3). The best chance for southern observers is in early February, when it lies in Capricornus (Star Map 7). There is no hope of seeing the Zodiacal Light or the Gegenschein except in the depth of the country, away from any source of illumination.

▼ **A diagram** to show how the Zodiacal Light appears in relation to the Sun.

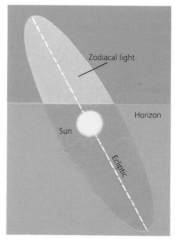

The Milky Way and Beyond

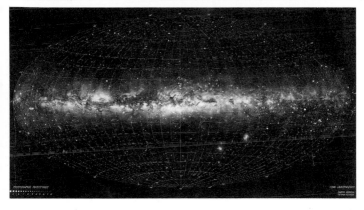

▲ **A photographic** 'panorama' of the Milky Way, as it might be seen by an astronaut out in space. The nucleus of the Galaxy is towards the centre, and the two small objects below it are our satellite galaxies, the Magellanic Clouds.

All the stars visible in the night sky belong to the Milky Way galaxy. Although it is such an obvious feature of a dark night sky, the Milky Way puzzled astronomers until well into the present century. It was known to consist of distant stars, but how distant – and what lay beyond? Was the Universe just an endless succession of stars? The problem could not be solved by direct observation, because our position inside it meant that its form could not be made out. The position was similar to being inside a group of people, unable to look over neighbouring heads to see how far it extends.

The clue came when astronomers began to study certain hazy objects in the sky that had previously been taken as clouds of gas and dust, or nebulae. They realized that some of these consisted of stars, so faint and close-packed that they must be very distant star-systems or galaxies. From this came the conclusion that the Milky Way was just one galaxy among many, and other galaxies could be used as prototypes to help classify it.

The Galaxy is a pinwheel-shaped spiral, like the Andromeda Galaxy two million light-years away. It is one of a group of over 30 that form a big cluster, the Local Group. Most of the galaxies in the Local Group are elliptical-shaped dwarfs, much smaller than the Milky Way. Our cluster measures about five million light-years across – not large compared with some groups, such as the Coma cluster which contains thousands of galaxies. Astronomers can make out the brighter individual stars in these neighbour galaxies, and they are similar to those in the Milky Way.

The Milky Way and Beyond

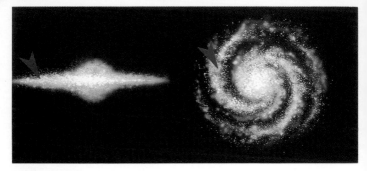

▲ **These two views** show how the Galaxy would appear if viewed from out in space. From edge-on the Galaxy looks like a flat disc with a swollen middle – the nucleus. From above, the Galaxy looks like a whirlpool of stars. The position of the Sun, and therefore our solar system, is indicated in both views by red arrows. The Galaxy contains upwards of 100,000 stars, but at least half of its material is in the form of non-luminous interstellar dust.

Galaxies in Space

Galaxies are scattered throughout space as far as telescopes can reach, but it is not easy to measure their distances. For many years, astronomers doubted whether any galaxies outside the Milky Way could be detected at all. For example, they thought M31 in Andromeda was a local star cluster.

But in the 1920s it was realized that M31 must be remote, since Cepheid variables were discovered in it, looking much fainter than the furthest Cepheids found in the Galaxy. Later on, novae were also found, and their assumed absolute magnitudes helped to place M31 at a distance of 2,200,000 light-years away.

Unfortunately, individual stars such as Cepheids and novae cannot be made out in very remote galaxies and other

methods must be used to measure their distance. One way is through the red-shift relationship (see page 152). Another is to make assumptions about the absolute magnitude of the whole galaxy. (The absolute magnitude of M31, for example, is about −21, equivalent in brightness to 25,000 million stars as luminous as the Sun.)

The difficulty with this method is that galaxies vary greatly in size and brightness. Some of the dwarf galaxies in the Local Group have absolute magnitudes as low as −9, which is not much brighter than a single highly-luminous supergiant star! Others are much more luminous than the Milky Way.

It seems that, although galaxies may differ greatly from one to another, the types of stars they contain can all be

found on the Milky Way-based Hertzsprung-Russell diagram. Star formation is a standard process throughout the universe.

▲ **The Whirlpool Galaxy** (above left) M51 was one of the first galaxies identified. The Andromeda Galaxy (above right), M31, is a bright nearby counterpart of the Milky Way.

▼ **M82 in Ursa Major,** an irregular galaxy about 8½ million light-years away. The Seyfert Galaxy (left) has an unusually bright nucleus

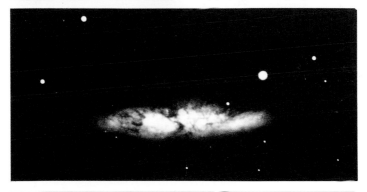

The Milky Way and Beyond

Classes of Galaxies

Tens of thousands of galaxies have been photographed in detail, and most fall into the following classes: spiral (normal and barred), elliptical (like a spiral's nucleus, without arms), and irregular.

The star populations in these classes differ considerably. Irregular galaxies such as the Magellanic Clouds contain many young stars and nebulae (from which more new stars can form). Spirals have a mixture of young and old stars. In the arms there are young, stars, Sun-like stars, dying white dwarfs and nebulae. In the nucleus are mostly old red giants.

Elliptical galaxies are the commonest type, and include some of the largest objects known, whose gravitational pull is 'sucking in' smaller galaxies. The stars are mainly red giants. There are also some very small examples, containing dim red stars: the faintest galaxies in the Local Group are of the elliptical class, as are the two bright satellite galaxies of M31 in Andromeda. The lack of dust and gas means that no new stars can be forming in these particular star systems.

▶ **The Magellanic Clouds** are visible to observers in the southern hemisphere.

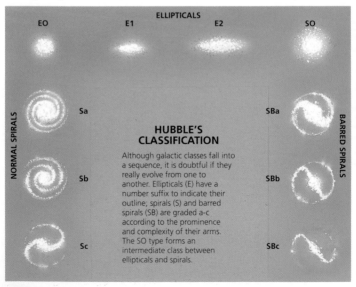

ELLIPTICALS

EO   E1   E2   SO

NORMAL SPIRALS

Sa

Sb

Sc

HUBBLE'S CLASSIFICATION

Although galactic classes fall into a sequence, it is doubtful if they really evolve from one to another. Ellipticals (E) have a number suffix to indicate their outline; spirals (S) and barred spirals (SB) are graded a-c according to the prominence and complexity of their arms. The SO type forms an intermediate class between ellipticals and spirals.

SBa

SBb

SBc

BARRED SPIRALS

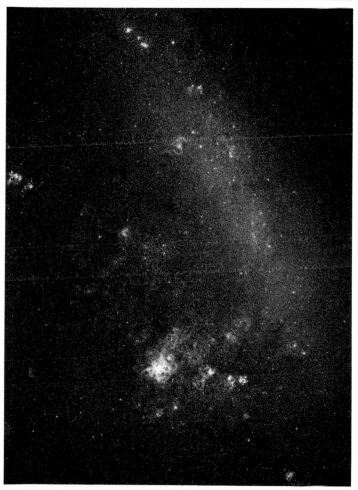

The Milky Way and Beyond

Observing Galaxies

Part of the fun of observing galaxies lies in the chase itself, for most are difficult to find and will be a challenge for the most careful observer. A dark, moonless night is essential for this work.

The sky notes on pages 76-90 give a good sample of the brighter galaxies, but only one in the whole sky, M31 in Andromeda, can be seen with the naked eye. If it happens to be well placed, spend some minutes examining it with binoculars or a small telescope. It may seem just a faint haze, but ask yourself the following questions, and others like them, and try to answer them accurately.

What shape is it? What direction is the long axis? What is the size in degrees or minutes of arc? How does the brightness change from centre to edge? Is the brightest part in the centre? Are there any dark or bright lanes, or condensations? Are any stars near it, or projected on it? Is any colour detectable? If seen, what does the satellite galaxy M32 look like?

When you look at *anything* in the sky, ask appropriate questions like these. Your eyes will respond, and your observing will improve.

The Origin of the Universe

Most astronomers accept the idea that the universe is expanding from the *Big Bang*. Galaxies are flying apart, and if their tracks are run backwards they must once have been very close together.

It might sound simple to work out when the expansion began, but astronomers disagree about how fast the galaxies are flying apart, and how far away they are. However, an age of at least 15 billion years was accepted by most astronomers until quite recently as the oldest stars seemed to be of this age.

The debate has now been opened by more accurate galaxy distance estimates, obtained using the Space Telescope. These suggest that the Universe is expanding more quickly than previously supposed, so that its age may only be between eight and 12 billion years. If this is so, either some other factors have not been taken into account, or the oldest stars in the Galaxy are younger than previously supposed.

Physicists have tried to analyse what must have happened to the material that gave rise to what we see now as the universe. If all the matter present now was present then, the 'primeval atom' must have been a mass of atomic particles at a temperature of *millions* of millions of degrees. Once it started expanding, however, the temperature would have dropped dramatically. Eventually, the chaos of particles must have started arranging itself into the elements we see today, hydrogen atoms being the simplest and by far the most common.

Evidence for the Big Bang theory comes from the discovery of faint radio waves that remain from the radiation pervading space. The only satisfactory explanation is that they represent the last traces of the primeval atom explosion, the flash of unbelievable heat that has almost faded away.

The Milky Way and Beyond

How the planets formed

The planets may have formed out of the 'doughnut' rather like this. Remember that on this scale of the Sun's diameter, the doughnut would be the size of a small garden.

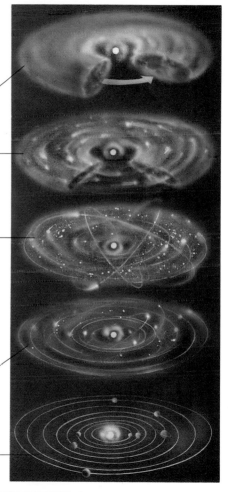

1 To begin with, the doughnut was a spinning ring of gas and dust.

2 The solid particles began to strike each other and stick together, forming larger bodies. At first, these were mostly carbon and ice.

3 These particles rapidly grew to planetary size. As they grew larger they began to 'pull' against each other, which meant that if they passed too close to each other, they were pulled into a different orbit. Some of the very small carbon-ice bodies were pulled so violently by the larger ones that they were thrown right out towards the stars, while others found themselves pulled into very long orbits that carried them far beyond the planets and back again very near to the Sun. These are the comets (see pages 138-141).

4 Eventually there were just a few large bodies going around the Sun in orbits that did not meet each other, and so there were no more collisions or near misses – the nine major planets were formed.

5 With the passages of thousands of millions of years the planets continued to pull against each other, until their orbits have become almost level.

The Milky Way and Beyond

Red-Shift

Light travels as tiny pulses moving through space at 300,000 kilometres per second. The colour of the light depends on the distance between the pulses, the *wavelength*. If a light source such as a star or galaxy is moving rapidly away from an observer, the wavelength is 'stretched'. A longer wavelength shifts the lines in the object's spectrum towards the red end, since red light has a longer wavelength than blue. All the clusters of galaxies in the night sky except those in the Local Group show red-shift and so indicate the expansion of the universe.

Those galaxies whose distances can be measured fairly accurately follow a law which says that the amount of red-shift of the spectral lines is proportional to their distance. In other words 'the farther, the faster'. If this law is correct, the red-shifts of very distant galaxies give a clue to their distance. The most remote objects so far observed are probably 10,000-15,000 million light-years away.

The 'Hubble constant' is somewhere in the region of 50-100 km/sec.

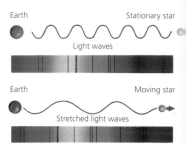

▲ **A shining body** emits electromagnetic radiation, which is energy pulses or waves. If it is moving at a high speed, its motion increases or decreases the wavelength as recorded by an observer.

Galaxy moving away from Earth

◀ **Many people** think that a receding galaxy appears red, but this is not the case. It is still seen through the eye's 'window' of white light, but the wavelength of the rays shining through that window now were beyond its limit when they left the galaxy. To a radio telescope on the Earth, their frequency (note) has been lowered.

▶ **Radio telescopes** are sensitive to long-wave electromagnetic radiation. This one, the 76-metre dish at Jodrell Bank, England, came into operation in 1955 as the first large steerable radio telescope in the world.

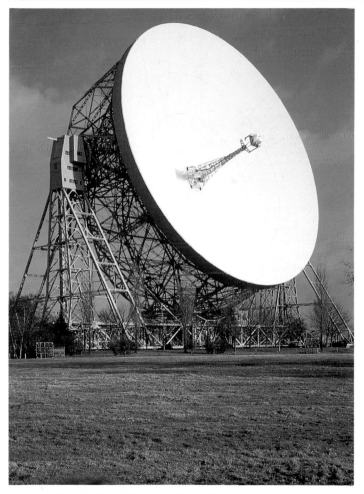

The Milky Way and Beyond

Pulsars and Quasars

Pulsars were detected in 1967 as faint regular pulses of radio signals, so brief and artificial-looking that they were once thought to be artificial messages.

Further work proved that they come from interstellar objects, some of which are spinning more than a hundred times a second. The only possible known candidate is a *neutron star*, the collapsed core of a supernova, in which the star's remaining material is compressed into a body only a few kilometres across. A pinhead of neutron-star material would weigh as much as a battleship. If our bodies were compressed into the solid atomic nuclear material they contain, we would be invisible without a microscope.

This was proved when the faint star at the centre of the Crab Nebula, the famous supernova remnant (page 55), was found to be pulsing at a high speed. The intense magnetic field of the star may be responsible for forcing its radiation into a narrow beam like that of a lighthouse.

Quasars

Quasars, or quasi-stellar objects, are the most powerful known energy-sources in the universe. They appear to be much smaller than ordinary galaxies (although there is considerable uncertainty about their size), but emit hundreds of times as much radiation.

The best explanation of a quasar is that a supermassive black hole at the centre of a galaxy causes material from the rest of the galaxy to swirl into it at almost the speed of light. This material would radiate energy on the scale observed. However, recent Space Telescope observations show that some quasars seem to be single brilliant objects with no surrounding gas and dust to 'fuel' them.

Beam of radiation rotates as star spins

Neutron star spins on axix

Radiation beam sent into space

▲ **The fierce radiation** from a spinning neutron star is squirted like water into two opposite narrow jets as its magnetic and gravitational fields intertwine. If the Earth lies in the plane of its spin, regular bursts of radiation will be detected.

▲ **These two photographs** reveal the pulsar at the centre of the Crab Nebula. It is alternately bright (left) and invisible (right) 30 times every second.

Large Red-Shifts

All quasars have very large red-shifts, which suggests that they are very far away; we are seeing them as they were thousands of millions of years ago, when the universe was younger than it is today. Perhaps they are short-lived objects that were formed early in the history of the universe.

Objects such as quasars and pulsars count among the most significant astronomical discoveries of the century. Just as the recent *Voyager* probes have made physicists puzzle over the nature of Saturn's rings, so the energy-production of quasars and the formation of pulsars have made scientists re-examine what they know about the nature of the physical world.

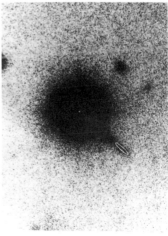

▲ **Quasar 3C 273,** about 600 million light-years away, is one of the closest and brightest known. (Negative print).

Simple Astrophotography

Astrophotography can be done without a telescope at all. Excellent star photographs can be taken using fast colour film such as Ektachrome 200 or 400, and any miniature camera with a lens opening of between f/2 and f/4. Black-and-white film, for example Kodak T-Max 400 or TP 2415, means that the processing can be done at home.

The star photographs on this spread were all taken in this way. The Pleiades picture opposite shows how much can be recorded with no special equipment, since most of these stars are hard to see or invisible with the naked eye. If the shutter is left open for a minute or less, the stars hardly have time to trail at all. Attaching the camera to an equatorially-mounted telescope means that much longer exposures can record pinpoint stars, like Coma Berenices (below).

▶ **The Pleiades** in the constellation Taurus, photographed with a stationary camera fitted with a telephoto lens. The Earth's rotation has made the stars drift during the exposure.

▲ **35-millimetre camera** ready to take time exposure of the sky. The cable release minimizes any shake as the shutter opens. The cardboard dew-cap also helps to keep away stray light.

▼ **The constellation** of Coma Berenices, photographed with a small camera guided to follow the stars.

Simple Astrophotography

Astrophotography with a Telescope

To take close-up pictures, the camera must be fitted to the telescope so that the image formed by the objective lens or mirror is focused sharply on the film.

You will need a camera with manual focusing and shutter: modern automatic cameras are not suitable for astrophotography. If you have a simple camera with a lens that cannot be removed, focus the telescope on an astronomical object and secure the camera behind the eyepiece, using cardboard, sticky tape, and a certain amount of ingenuity, without altering the focus. In theory this will produce a sharp image, although it will be advisable to take several exposures, slightly altering and recording the telescope's focus each time, selecting the best setting after developing the pictures.

If the camera lens can be removed, and the camera has a focal-plane shutter, the image formed by the telescope's lens or mirror can be focused directly on the film. This method is ideal for images of the Sun or Moon where most or all of the disc is to be recorded. Using medium-speed film, an exposure of about 1/50th of a second with a Newtonian refractor, and about 1/10th of a second with a refractor, is a good choice for the Moon at half-phase. The full Moon will require only a quarter of the exposure, the crescent twice as much.

Exposures must be shorter than about half a second, or the Earth's rotation will noticeably blur the image. In the case of the Sun, the difficulty is to make the exposure short enough. Special aluminized plastic filters are available that fit over the telescope aperture, reducing the light intensity to a tiny fraction of its original strength.

To obtain a larger image, use an

◀ **A medium-sized** refracting telescope with a camera attached for direct photography of the sky. The four pictures of the Moon on page 94 were taken in this way, with exposures of about one second.

eyepiece between the telescope's image and the camera. This amplifies the image and allows more detail to be recorded.

All the planets except Venus require longer exposures than the Moon, and their images are so small that eyepiece magnification is essential. In future, video recording is certain to make some traditional fields of astrophotography obsolete, and planetary photography is one of these. Video cameras are far more sensitive than photographic emulsions, images can be stored or rejected as they are taken, and can later be 'processed' to bring out more detail.

▶ **This equatorially-mounted** reflecting telescope of 150 millimetres aperture is very suitable for taking photographs of the Moon and brighter planets. It can also be used as a guide telescope for a 35mm camera.

◀ **The Moon's surface** offers plenty of challenges for astrophotographers. This picture shows craters in the southern hemisphere.

▼ **To take successful** pictures of the Sun, a very dense filter is necessary. The photograph below shows the solar disc as it appeared on August 24, 1990.

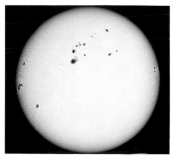

A Sky Diary

This Diary records just some of the interesting events in the sky between 1995 and 2000. All times are GMT. (If you want to observe other minima of Algol the times can be calculated by knowing that its exact cycle of brightness change takes 68h 49m). More detailed predictions can be found in astronomical yearbooks such as *The B.A.A. Handbook* (see page 172).

1995

Jan 3 (Tue) Quadrantid meteor shower at maximum, 14.00. Very favourable: New Moon.

Jan 13 (Fri) Venus at morning elongation.

Jan 19 (Thu) Mercury at evening elongation, favourable for northern observers.

Feb 12 (Sun) Mars at opposition in Leo, magnitude – 1.0.

Mar 1 (Wed) Mercury at morning elongation, favourable for southern observers.

Apr 15 (Sat) Partial eclipse of the Moon, 12.16 (see page 96).

Apr 21 (Fri) Lyrid meteor shower at maximum, 22.00. Fairly favourable: Moon at Last Quarter.

May 22 (Mon) The Earth passes through the plane of Saturn's rings (north to south).

June 1 (Thu) Jupiter at opposition in Ophiuchus, magnitude – 2.1.

Aug 11 (Fri) The Earth passes through the plane of Saturn's rings (south to north).

Aug 12 (Sat) Persied meteor shower at maximum, 10.00. Unfavourable: Full Moon.

Sep 9 (Sat) Mercury at evening elongation, favourable for southern observers.

Sep 14 (Thu) Saturn at opposition in Aquarius, magnitude 0.9.

Oct 20 (Fri) Mercury at morning elongation, favourable for northern observers.

Oct 24 (Tue) Eclipse of the Sun (see page 39).

Dec 14 (Thu) Geminid meteor shower at maximum, 10.00. Fairly favourable: Moon at Last Quarter.

Dec 22 (Fri) Algol at minimum brightness, 21.30.

1996

Jan 3 (Wed) Quadrantid meteor shower at maximum, 19.00. Unfavourable: Full Moon.

Feb 11 (Sun) Mercury at morning elongation, favourable for southern observers.

Feb 12 (Mon) The Earth passes through the plane of Saturn's rings (north to south).

Apr 1 (Mon) Venus at evening elongation.

Apr 4 (Thu) Total eclipse of the Moon, 00.07 (see page 96).

Apr 21 (Sun) Lyrid meteor shower at maximum, 02.00. Favourable: waxing crescent Moon.

Apr 23 (Tue) Mercury at evening elongation, favourable for northern observers.

Jul 4 (Thu) Jupiter at opposition in Sagittarius, magnitude 02.2.

Aug 11 (Sun) Perseid meteor shower at maximum, 19.00. Favourable: New Moon.

Aug 19 (Mon) Venus at morning elongation.

Aug 21 (Wed) Mercury at evening elongation, favourable for southern observers.

Sep 26 (Thu) Saturn at opposition in Pisces, magnitude 0.7.

Sep 27 (Fri) Total eclipse of the Moon, 02.51 (see page 96).

Oct 3 (Thu) Mercury at morning elongation, favourable for northern observers.

Dec 2 (Mon) Algol at minimum brightness, 20.13.

Dec 13 (Fri) Geminid meteor shower at maximum, 14.00. Favourable: waxing crescent Moon.

1997

Jan 3 (Fri) Quadrantid meteor shower at maximum. 02.00. Fairly favourable: Moon at Last Quarter.

Mar 8-9 (Sat) Eclipse of the Sun (see page 39).

Mar 17 (Mon) Mars at opposition in Virgo, magnitude 0.9.

Apr 6 (Sun) Mercury at evening elongation, favourable for northern observers.

Apr 21 (Mon) Lyrid shower at maximum, 10.00. Unfavourable: Full Moon.

Aug 9 (Sat) Jupiter at opposition in Capricornus, magnitude 2.4.

Aug 12 (Tue) Perseid meteor shower at maximum, 05.00. Favourable: Moon at First Quarter.

Sep 16 (Tue) Mercury at morning elongation, favourable for northern observers.

Sep 16 (Tue) Total eclipse of the Moon, 13.35 (see page 96).

Oct 10 (Fri) Saturn at opposition in Pisces, magnitude 0.4.

Nov 6 (Thu) Venus at evening elongation.

Nov 28 (Fri) Mercury at evening elongation, favourable for southern observers.

Dec 4 (Thu) Algol at minimum brightness, 20.37.

Dec 13 (Sat) Geminid meteor shower at maximum, 19.00. Unfavourable: Full Moon.

1998

Jan 3 (Sat) Quadrantid meteor shower at maximum, 17.00. Fairly favourable: Moon at First Quarter.

Feb 26 (Thu) Total eclipse of the Sun (see page 39).

Mar 20 (Fri) Mercury at evening elongation, favourable for northern observers.

Mar 27 (Fri) Venus at morning elongation, favourable for northern observers.

Apr 22 (Wed) Lyrid meteor shower at maximum, 00.00. Fairly favourable: Moon at Last Quarter.

May 4 (Mon) Mercury at morning elongation, favourable for southern observers.

Aug 12 (Wed) Perseid meteor shower at maximum, 08.00. Unfavourable: gibbous Moon.

Aug 31 (Mon) Mercury at morning elongation, favourable for northern observers.

Sep 16 (Wed) Jupiter at opposition in Pisces.

Oct 23 (Fri) Saturn at opposition in Aries.

Nov 11 (Wed) Mercury at evening elongation, favourable for southern observers.

Dec 8 (Tue) Algol at minimum brightness, 22.32.

Dec 13 (Sun) Geminid meteor at maximum, 14.00. Favourable: crescent Moon.

1999

Jan 3 (Sun) Quadrantid meteor shower at maximum, 23.00. Unfavourable: Full Moon.

Mar 3 (Wed) Mercury at evening elongation, favourable for northern observers.

Apr 16 (Fri) Mercury at morning elongation, favourable for southern observers.

Apr 22 (Thu) Lyrid meteor shower at maximum, 06.00. Fairly favourable: Moon at First Quarter.

Apr 24 (Sat) Mars at opposition in Virgo.

June 11 (Fri) Venus at evening elongation.

Jul 28 (Wed) Partial eclipse of the Moon, 11.25 (see page 96).

Aug 11 (Wed) Total eclipse of the Sun visible in England (see page 39).

Aug 12 (Thu) Perseid meteor shower at maximum, 05.00. Favourable: New Moon.

Aug 14 (Sat) Mercury at morning elongation, favourable for morning observers.

Oct 23 (Sat) Jupiter at opposition in Aries.

Oct 24 (Sun) Mercury at evening elongation, favourable for southern observers.

Oct 31 (Sat) Venus at morning elongation.

Nov 6 (Sat) Saturn at opposition in Aries.

Dec 6 (Mon) Algol at minimum brightness, 22.09.

Dec 14 (Tues) Geminid meteor shower at maximum, 00.00. Favourable: crescent Moon.

2000

Jan 4 (Tue) Quadrantid meteor shower at maximum, 05.00. Favourable: New Moon.

Jan 21 (Fri) Total eclipse of the Moon, 04.40 (see page 96).

Feb 15 (Tue) Mercury at evening elongation, favourable for northern observers.

Mar 28 (Tue) Mercury at morning elongation, favourable for southern observers.

Apr 21 (Fri) Lyrid meteor shower at maximum, 10.00. Unfavourable: gibbous Moon.

Aug 11 (Fri) Perseid meteor shower at maximum, 18.00. Fairly favourable: gibbous Moon.

Oct 6 (Fri) Mercury at evening elongation, favourable for southern observers.

Nov 15 (Wed) Mercury at morning elongation, favourable for northern observers.

Nov 19 (Sun) Saturn at opposition in Taurus.

Nov 28 (Tue) Jupiter at opposition in Taurus.

Dec 6 (Wed) Algol at minimum brightness, 18.35.

Dec 13 (Wed) Geminid meteor shower at maximum, 02.00. Unfavourable: Full Moon.

Key Dates in Astronomical History

BC

c.3000 Babylonian astronomical records begin.

c.1000 Chinese astronomical records begin.

c.280 Aristarchus suggests that the Earth orbits the Sun.

c.270 Eratosthenes makes an accurate estimate of the size of the Earth.

c.130 Hipparchus draws up the first star catalogue.

AD

c.140 Ptolemy's *Almagest* written; his Earth-centred universe accepted.

903 Star positions measured by Al-Sufi.

1054 Supernova in Taurus recorded by Chinese astronomers.

1433 Ulugh Beigh's star catalogue compiled.

1543 Nicolaus Copernicus proposes a Sun-centred system.

1572 Supernova in Cassiopeia observed by Tycho Brahe.

1600 Johannes Kepler starts analysing Tycho's planetary observations and derives his three laws of planetary motion (1609-1618).

1608 The refracting telescope invented by Hans Lippershey.

1609 Galileo and others make the first telescopic observations.

1631 Transit of Mercury across the Sun, predicted by Kepler, is observed by Gassendi.

1638 Holwarda discovers the famous variable star Mira Ceti.

1647 One of the first lunar maps is drawn by Hevelius.

1668 Isaac Newton constructs the first reflecting telescope.

1687 Newton's *Principia*, containing his theory of gravitation is published.

1705 Edmond Halley predicts that the comet last seen in 1682 will return again in 1758.

1725 The first 'modern' star catalogue, based on Flamsteed's observations, published.

1758 John Dollond manufactures the first successful achromatic object-glass. Halley's comet makes its predicted return.

1761 The first transit of Venus across the Sun observed.

1781 William Herschel discovers the new planet Uranus, and Charles Messier publishes his catalogue of star clusters and nebulae.

1801 Giuseppe Piazzi discovers the first asteroid, Ceres.

▼ **Astronomers** in Istanbul Observatory in the Middle Ages. Notice the astronomical instruments they used.

Key Dates in Astronomical History

1834 Bessel discovers the first white dwarf star, the companion of Sirius.

1838 Friedrich Wilhelm Bessel makes the first interstellar distance measurement, of 61 Cygni.

1840 The first astronomical photograph, of the Moon, taken by John William Draper.

1843 The sunspot cycle announced by Samuel Heinrich Schwabe.

1846 Neptune discovered as a result of predictions by John Couch Adams and Urbain Leverrier.

1859 Gustav Kirchhoff proves that the elements in a hot body imprint characteristic lines in its spectrum.

1863 Secchi makes pioneer observations of the spectra of stars and divides them into 'families'.

1870-1900 Great developments in astronomical photography and spectrum analysis.

1877 Legendary opposition of Mars, when Schiaparelli announced that he had discovered channels ('canals').

1891 George Ellery Hale invents spectroheliograph for photographing the Sun at a single wavelength.

1908 The Hertzsprung-Russell diagram introduces the idea of giant and dwarf stars. The first of the 'giant' reflecting telescopes, the 1.5 metre at Mount Wilson, begins work.

1912 The Cephid period-luminosity law announced by Henrietta Leavitt.

1920 The red-shift first noticed in distant galaxies.

1923 Edwin Powell Hubble makes the first good measurement of the distance of M31 in Andromeda.

1930 Clyde Tombaugh discovers Pluto.

1930-1960 Many investigations into stellar energy production and the evolution of stars.

1937 The first radio waves from space detected by Grote Reber.

1948 The Mount Palomar 5-metre reflector completed.

1955 The Jodrell Bank 76-metre radio telescope completed.

1963 The great distances of quasars established. Background radiation pervading space discovered.

1967 Pulsars discovered by Jocelyn Bell and Anthony Hewish. Moon's independence assured under the United Nations Treaty on Outer Space.

1987 Supernova observed in the Greater Magellanic Cloud.

1992 The first object orbiting beyond Pluto discovered. About 200 km across, it is known as 1992QB1.

1994 Comet Shoemaker-Levy 9 crashes into Jupiter.

1995 NASA releases the 'Deep Field' images from the Hubble Space Telescope; revealing no less than 1,500 galaxies at various stages of development.

2001 International team discover 11 distant planets. Number of known planets (outside solar system) rises to 63.

Key Dates in Space Exploration

1804 The first high-altitude ascent made by Gay-Lussac and Biot in a hot-air balloon, reaching a height of seven kilometres.

1896 Unmanned balloons, launched by Teisserenc de Bort, analyse the atmosphere at heights of up to 15 kilometres.

1903 Ziolkovsky proposes a rocket-propelled spacecraft.

1919 Goddard publishes a monograph on rocket propulsion.

1923 Oberth's book *The Rocket into Interplanetary Space* published.

1926 Goddard launches the first liquid-fuelled rocket.

1942 Experiments with the V2 rocket at Peenemunde achieve heights of 180 kilometres.

1949 The first two-stage rocket, the WAC-Corporal, achieves a height of 400 kilometres.

1950 Cape Canaveral first used for rocket experiments.

1955 The USA announces its intention of launching space satellites.

1957 The world's first satellite, *Sputnik* 1, launched by the USSR on October 4.

1958 *Explorer* 1, the first satellite launched by the USA, discovers radiation belts around the Earth.

1959 Three lunar probes launched by the USSR: *Lunar* 3 photographs the far side; *Lunar* 2 hits the surface.

1961 The first manned orbital flight, by USSR astronaut Gagarin in *Vostok*.

1962 The first successful inter-planetary probe, *Mariner* 2, sends back information about Venus.

1964 The first close-up pictures of the Moon obtained by *Ranger* 7 (USA).

1965 *Mariner* 4 (USA) passes Mars and transmits pictures and information.

1966 *Venera* 3 (USSR) lands on Venus, the first spacecraft to reach another planet. *Luna* 9 (USSR) makes the first soft landing on the Moon, followed by *Surveyor* 1 (USA). The first of the *Orbiter* mapping lunar satellites launched (USA).

1967 *Venera* 4 (USSR) soft-lands on Venus and sends back information.

1969 *Mariner* 6 and 7 (USA) pass Mars and send back pictures and information. *Apollo* 11 lands the first men on the Moon (July 20).

1970 The first automatic lunar probe, *Luna* 16 (USSR), returns a sample to Earth.

1971 *Mariner* 9 (USA) goes into orbit around Mars and sends back a great deal of information.

1972 The last manned mission to the Moon, in *Apollo* 17.

1973 The first flyby of Jupiter, by *Pioneer* 10, which becomes the first man-made artifact to escape from the Solar System. *Skylab*, an orbiting astronomical laboratory, launched by the USA and visited by three different teams.

1974 *Mariner* 10 (USA) passes both Venus and Mercury. *Salyut* 3 and 4 (USSR) link up to form orbiting observatory. *Pioneer* 11 (USA) passes Jupiter and heads for Saturn.

1976 The first successful landings on Mars by the two *Viking* craft (USA).

1977 *Voyagers* 1 and 2 launched towards the outer planets.

1978 *Pioneer Venus* project (USA) puts two craft into orbit around Venus and lands four surface probes.

Key Dates in Space Exploration

1979 *Voyagers* 1 and 2 (USA) pass Jupiter. *Pioneer* 11 passes Saturn successfully after a six-year journey.

1980 *Voyager* 1 makes successful flyby of Saturn, and heads for outer space.

1981 The first space shuttle, *Columbia* (USA), completes two flights. *Voyager* 2 passes Saturn.

1982 USSR send probe to Venus.

1986 The space shuttle *Challenger* explodes at take-off. *Voyager* 2 sends back photographs of Uranus and its moons. The *Giotto* space probe passes through Halley's comet. The core modul of the Russian Space Station *Mir* launched.

1989 *Voyager* 2 passes Neptune, its last planetary target.

1990 Hubble Space Telescope launched. *Magellan* probe goes into orbit around Venus; maps most of surface of Venus by means of radar; the Cosmic Background Explorer satellite examines the Big Bang background radiation.

1991 The *Galileo* Jupiter probe obtains the first close-up view of an asteroid.

1992 NASA begins the 10-year SETI project to search for extra-terrestrial radio transmissions.

1993 Contact lost with the *Mars Observer* spacecraft just three days before it was due to go into orbit around the planet.

1994 After a Shuttle repair mission, the Hubble Space Telescope performance is greatly improved.

1995 *Galileo* orbits Jupiter and transmits pictures and data. First rendezvous of a NASA spacecraft with *Mir*.

1997 *Mars Pathfinder* parachutes down to Mars and analyses Martian rocks for 3 months. *Cassini* launched and due to reach Saturn's orbit by 2004. NASA extends the Hubble Space Telescope's operations from 2005 to 2010.

1998 The first part of the International Space Station launched. The ISS due for completion by 2004.

1999 Fourth gyroscope on the Hubble Space Telescope fails. No longer able to aim it shuts down to wait for repairs. *Stardust* probe launched to intercept Comet *Wild 2* and return sample material by 2006.

2000 $12.5 million donated to allow SETI to build the world's most powerful instrument to listen for radio signals from other life in the galaxy. Project to be in full operation by 2005.

2001 Space tourist Dennis Tito pays $20 million for an eight-day visit to the ISS. *Mir* falls to Earth: its life over. NASA selects Lockhead Martin to construct the 2005 Mars craft. The craft will return the highest resolution images ever taken by a Mars-circling orbiter.

▶ **An American astronaut** leans out into space, whilst anchored to a remote manipulator system (RMS).

Glossary

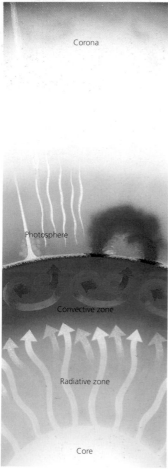

Corona

Photosphere

Convective zone

Radiative zone

Core

Not all these words are used in the book but they are useful terms and ones that you may come across as an amateur astronomer.

Absorption spectrum Spectrum crossed by dark lines due to light absorbed by intervening cool gas.

Achromatic lens Used in a refracting telescope to give a colour-free image. A non-achromatic lens produces false colour fringes around objects in the sky.

Aerolite A meteorite consisting mainly of stony material.

Airglow Faint auroral luminosity of the night sky.

Albedo The ratio of light reflected to light received.

Altitude The height of an object above the horizon, measured in degrees (°).

Aphelion The point on the orbit of a planetary body that is farthest from the Sun.

Apogee The point on the orbit of a satellite that is farthest from the planet.

Astronomical Unit The mean distance of the Earth from the Sun (149,597,870 kilometres).

Binary Star A pair of stars orbiting around each other.

Chromosphere The inner atmosphere of the Sun.

Coma The head of a comet.

Comes The faint companion of a double star.

Conjunction Occurs when a planet, the Earth and the Sun are in line. In the case of Mercury and Venus which can come between the Earth and the Sun, they are said to be at inferior conjunction on the near side of the Sun and at superior conjunction on the far side.

Corona The Sun's outer atmosphere. ◄

Declination A co-ordinate for finding objects in the sky. The equivalent of latitude on Earth.

Dichotomy The half-phase of the Moon or a planet.

Doppler shift The change of wavelength of sound or light waves due to motion between the source and the observer.

Eccentricity The word used to describe the difference between an ellipse and a circle. A very eccentric ellipse is a long thin loop.

Ecliptic is the path followed by the Sun around the year.

Ellipse The oval path traced by the planets and many comets.

Elongation The angle of Mercury or Venus from the Sun at any given time.

Emission spectrum Spectrum of bright lines, caused by luminous gas.

Eyepiece The lens or group of lenses in a telescope against which the eye is placed. It magnifies the image made by the object glass or mirror.

Fireball A meteor brighter than the planet Venus. ▲

Focal length The distance between a lens or mirror and the image it forms of a remote object.

Fraunhöfer lines The absorption lines in the solar spectrum.

Galaxy A star system. The Galaxy refers to the galaxy to which our Sun belongs. ▼

TYPES OF GALAXY

Irregular galaxies

Elliptical galaxies

Ordinary spiral galaxies

Barred spiral galaxies

Glossary

Gegenschein A very faint permanent glow in the sky opposite the Sun.

Granulation The fine mottled texture of the Sun's surface.

Hour angle The time in sidereal hours between a celestial object's present position and its meridian transit.

Ionosphere The upper layer of the Earth's atmosphere (above about 70 kilometres) where most atoms have either lost or gained electrons, and are therefore ionised.

Light-year Distance travelled by light in a year (9,460,700,000,000 kilometres).

Limb The edge of the Sun, Moon or a planet as it is seen in the sky.

Luminosity A measure of light produced by a star.

Lunation The interval from one New Moon to the next.

Magnitude A scale that measures the brightness of a star.

Magnetosphere The shell of charged particles held around the Earth by its magnetic field.

Meridian An imaginary line crossing the sky and passing through zenith and the North and South celestial poles.

Midnight Sun The presence of the Sun above the horizon at midnight in high latitudes, when its distance from the celestial pole is smaller than the pole's altitude.

Node The point at which the orbit of the Moon or a planet crosses the plane of the Earth's orbit (ecliptic).

Occultation The covering of a celestial body by the Moon or a planet.

Opposition The instant when a planet is opposite in the sky to the Sun.

Parallax The slight shift in the position of a nearby star when viewed from opposite sides of the Earth's orbit.

Periastron The closest approach of two stars in a binary system as seen from the Earth.

Perigee The point on the orbit of a satellite that is closest to the planet.

Perihelion The point on the orbit of a planetary body that is closest to the Sun.

Perturbation The departure of a body from its true course due to the gravitational pull of another body.

Photosphere The visible surface of the Sun.

Prominence Eruptions of gas from the surface of the Sun. ▼

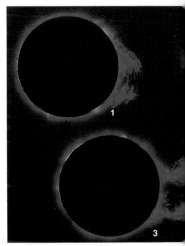

▲ Four stages in the eruption and decay of a huge solar prominence, recorded by a space-borne telescope over a period of two days.

Proper motion Drift of a star across the celestial sphere due to its own motion.

Radial velocity Motion of a star or galaxy towards or away from the observer.

Red-shift The way in which a star's colour reddens when it moves rapidly away from the observer. An approaching object becomes bluer, showing blue shift.

Retrograde motion Motion in the opposite sense from that followed by the planets in their orbits (anti-clockwise as seen from the north).

Saros The interval of 18 years 103 days, after which the Sun, Moon and Earth are in almost exactly the same relative position, and eclipses will recur.

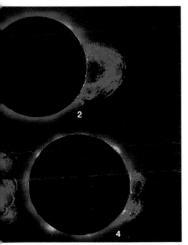

Sidereal day The time taken by the Earth to rotate once as measured by a star: 23 hours, 56 minutes and 4 seconds long.

Siderite A meteorite consisting mainly of iron.

Solar day The time taken by the Earth to rotate once as measured by the Sun: 24 hours.

Solar wind The continuous outflow of atomic particles from the Sun.

Spectroheliograph An instrument for photographing the Sun in the light emitted by a single element.

Stratosphere The layer of calm, cold air lying between 15 and 40 kilometres above the Earth's surface. ▼

Tektites Small glassy bodies, probably caused by material thrown up when meteorites hit the Earth long ago.

Transit The passage of a smaller body across the disc of a larger one.

Troposphere The lower region of the Earth's atmosphere, extending to a height of about 15 kilometres. ▼

Wavelength The distance between pulses of radiation.

Wolf-Rayet stars Very hot stars with luminous atmospheres.

Zenithal Hourly Rate (ZHR) The number of meteors per hour that would be seen if the radiant were at the zenith.

Zodiacal Band An excessively faint band of light extending around the ecliptic caused by interplanetary particles reflecting sunlight.

▼ The troposphere contains most of the Earth's atmosphere, but traces of air are still found several hundred kilometres above the surface

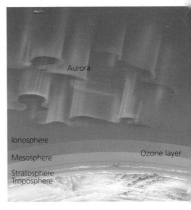

Societies and Useful books

If you want to find out more about astronomy, the best way of going about it is to join a local society. Societies are always on the lookout for new members, particularly for enthusiasts who want to learn.

You will have the chance of looking through powerful telescopes, of borrowing books from the library (most societies have one), and of getting advice.

This is the most important benefit of all. You will probably find someone who has done astrophotography, someone else who has observed variable stars, and so on...and you will learn far more by asking them questions than you will from books alone.

Ask at the local library or the civic centre if there is a society in your area; or else write to the **Federation of Astronomical Societies**, 10 Glan y Llyn, North Cornelly, Bridgend County Borough, Wales, CF33 4EF (www.fedastro.org.uk).

The Society for Popular Astronomy (36 Fairway, Keyworth, Nottingham, NG12 5DU) issues a quarterly journal, *Popular Astronomy*, which includes predictions of occultations, variable stars, and planet movements. The Society - for beginners of all ages - holds meetings and residential courses (www.popastro.com).

The senior amateur society in the UK is the **British Astronomical Association** (Burlington House,

Piccadilly, London, W1J 0DU (www.ast.cam.ac.uk)), which was founded in 1890 and has a tremendous record of observational work.

Books to Read

The following books contain a great deal of useful information for the practical amateur:

Yearbooks and Atlases

The BAA Handbook obtainable from the British Astronomical Association (address above).

Yearbook of Astronomy edited by Patrick Moore (Sidgwick & Jackson, annually).

Norton's Star Atlas and Reference Handbook (Longman, 1998) is the best star atlas.

Guidebooks

Philip's Guide to the Night Sky by Patrick Moore (Philip, 1996).

The Urban Astronomer by Gregory Matloff (Wiley, 1991).

Exploring the Night Sky with Binoculars by Patrick Moore (Cambridge University Press, 2000).

► **The Hubble Space Telescope**, launched in 1990, orbits the Earth's surface and uses a mirror 2.4m across.

Index

Index

Index

Acknowledgements

Photographs: Page 8 Kitt Peak Observatory; 11 Galaxy Picture Library; 15 Long & Wood; 20 Galaxy Picture Library; 77 Galaxy Picture Library; 87 Californian Institute of Technology; 94 Galaxy Picture Library; 94 Galaxy Picture Library; 97 Galaxy Picture Library; 99 Galaxy Picture Library; 101 Galaxy Picture Library; 113 Jet Propulsion Laboratory; 118 New Mexico State University; 125 NASA; 12 Jet Propulsion Laboratory; 130 Jet Propulsion Laboratory; 131 Jet Propulsion Laboratory; 132 Galaxy Picture Library; 147 Jet Propulsion Laboratory; 155 & 156 Royal Astronomical Society; 157 Galaxy Picture Library; 159 Galaxy Picture Library; 163 & 164 NASA.

All other photographs Science Photo Library.